SHORT CUTS

INTRODUCTIONS TO FILM STUDIES

CINEMA AND HISTORY

THE TELLING OF STORIES

MIKE CHOPRA-GANT

WALLFLOWER

LONDON and NEW YORK

First published in Great Britain in 2008 by
Wallflower Press
6 Market Place, London W1W 8AF
www.wallflowerpress.co.uk

A catalogue record for this book is available from the British Library

ISBN 978 1 905674 59 6

Series design by Rob Bowden Design

Printed in Great Britain by Antony Rowe, Chippenham, Wiltshire

CONTENTS

ACKNOWLEDGEMENTS

Although writing a book is often a solitary endeavour it would be impossible without the generous help and support of family, friends and colleagues. Numerous people have contributed to this book. Without the support of the Media, Culture and Communications Research Capability Fund Committee at London Metropolitan University – Bill Osgerby, Paul Cobley and Wendy Wheeler – and that of Anna Gough-Yates, I would still be writing. My thanks to you all. Thanks too go to Gholam Khiabany and Milly Williamson who managed to occasionally drag me away from writing and gave me some semblance of a social life. But my greatest gratitude is reserved for my wife Pam and our two wonderful children, Keshika and Umika, who gave unconditional love and support and who always make me smile.

INTRODUCTION: FILM HISTORY AFTER THE 'END OF HISTORY'

In the spring of 1994 the journal *Film History* published a special edition dedicated to the philosophy of film history. The essays collected in the volume sought to address some of the fundamental questions raised by attempts to employ the array of methods and analytical approaches that are commonly grouped together under the collective term 'history', as a way of understanding film. The editor provided a clear statement of the key questions that the volume would address: 'what are the rules, methods, research criteria and inspiring principles involved in the practice of exploring the past of cinema?' (Usai 1994: 3). Readers who have never encountered history above secondary school level are likely to regard this degree of attention to the concept of history with some bemusement. Surely history is an unproblematic idea, a simple record of events that happened in the past, a series of 'facts' about the past? Even at higher levels of study, although students are unlikely to accept unquestioningly an over-simplified view of history as an unmediated series of events or 'facts' relating to the past, the wide range of potential meanings encompassed by this deceptively simple concept may equally bewilder them. As Paolo Cherchi Usai noted later in his editorial, none of the contributors to this issue of the journal was attempting to produce a totalising definition of film history, but instead recognised that it is a multi-faceted area of academic study likely to produce 'a baffling – although potentially fertile – galaxy of non-mutually exclusive options' (ibid.) rather than an exhaustive (and necessarily reductive) account of the past of cinema or cinema's relationship with the past. History, then, is a complicated idea that cannot be encapsulated in a singular, definitive account that represents the only possible interpretation to be given to a set of 'facts'; and it becomes more complicated when film is brought into the mix, because film is neither the type of 'document' of earlier periods that historians are accustomed to working with, nor the traditional medium with which historians have informed us about the past.

The aim of this book is to consider some of the ways that film and history come into contact with one another. In particular it will look at two aspects of this: first, how films can be used as a form of evidence of the discourses, attitudes and values prevalent in a culture at the time they were created and released and, second, at how filmmakers have used the past in the telling of their stories. The book will demonstrate what can be gained by looking at films through the lens of history, what subtle nuances of meaning it is possible to detect by using a historical approach as opposed to any of the more abstract, theoretical approaches available to film scholars. Finally the book aims, through the use of detailed case studies, to demonstrate how historical analysis of films can be undertaken; what methods and resources can be used to ground an analysis of a film in an empirical, historical base. However, because history is such a complicated concept this is less straightforward than it might first appear.

A few years ago the very idea of history appeared to be under threat of extinction from a rash of postmodern theory that was coming to prominence in both scholarly and popular discourses. One prominent writer, Francis Fukuyama, famously declared in 1989 that we had reached the 'end of history'. Although Fukuyama has subsequently been at pains to insist that his was not a general declaration that history had ceased to exist, the idea that, at least in the capitalist democracies of the West, we had entered a new post-historical era was palpable in the writing of numerous other thinkers. Approaching history from the other end of the political spectrum from Fukuyama, Fredric Jameson also discerned a 'weakening of historicity' (1991: 6) in the late-capitalist cultures of the Western democracies. This, argued Jameson, lent those cultures a 'schizophrenic' quality in which much of our sense of temporality was lost in a culture in which the superficial manifestations of all past eras were resurrected in an atemporal present (see 1991: 279–96). What the claims of thinkers such as Fukuyama and Jameson demonstrate is that the idea of history is far from the straightforward assemblage of 'facts' encountered in high-school history lessons; history is itself a contestable category and the pursuit of historical study involves engagement with epistemological and methodological questions that are anything but straightforward.

So far as the study of film up to that time was concerned there was much that seemed to support Fukuyama's suggestion of history's obsolescence. From the early days of academic film studies a split developed between scholars with a historical view of film and those whose view of film was conditioned by literary theories.[1] These latter film theorists sought to interpret films by inserting them into theoretical frameworks rather than considering the historico-social contexts in which films were produced, watched and enjoyed by audiences. Of the two, it is the latter theoretical approach that tended to dominate during the 1970s and 1980s. Among the effects of this abstract approach to film were a professionalisation and institutionalisation of the appreciation of film, and the production of esoteric and theoretically dense 'readings' of films that often exhibit, at best, a simple disinterest in film's social and historical dimensions and, at worst, a view of film that is so radically alienated from any context other than the theoretical framework within which the film has been interpreted that any sense that films exist within material historico-social contexts almost disappeared entirely. This dichotomy between abstract, theoretical approaches, on the one hand, and more empirical, historical approaches on the other, still exists to some extent and remains the subject of much debate in film studies today. In recent years, however, there has been a discernible resurgence of interest in the historical study of film and cinema, and today the historical study of film has never been more relevant.

This book is intended as an introductory text and the account of film and history contained in it necessarily represents a starting point for students' deeper engagement with film and cinema history rather than an attempt to give an exhaustive account of every aspect of this area of study. The book focuses on certain key aspects of the relationship between film and history and, where appropriate, signals the existence of other accounts that deal with different aspects of that relationship. It will not attempt to provide easy answers to some of the difficult issues that arise when considering film and history. Nor is it partisan, taking sides with one or other of the opposing camps of thinkers. Instead the book will draw on the strengths of several approaches – including the empiricism of traditional, 'scientific' historians and the understanding of the role of discourse in shaping our understanding of the world, advanced by postmodern literary theorists and historians – in order to demonstrate the interplay between 'facts' of history and the discourses within which those raw 'facts' become meaningful. First, however, it is necessary to think about what is meant by film history.

What is (Film) History?

The historical study of films and cinema is a specialised sub-branch of cultural history, itself a sub-branch of history in general. As such, while many of the issues at stake in film history are unique to this particular branch of historical enquiry, many others arise in all areas of historical study. In *What is History?* E. H. Carr provides one of the most intelligent and accessible commentaries on the nature of historical inquiry. According to Carr, history does not consist of an objective and irreducible set of 'facts' about the past. While 'facts' are an element in the process of writing history, these facts can never be taken at face value: 'facts speak only when the historian calls on them: it is he who decides to which facts to give the floor, and in what order and context' (1990: 11). Before they are able to 'speak', however, these facts have to overcome various obstacles to becoming part of history. It is inconceivable that a historian will have access to all of the facts about a past event. Documents are lost and memories fade, leaving history looking like 'an enormous jig-saw with a lot of missing parts' (1990: 13). Histories are, therefore, inevitably based on a partial set of 'facts'.

Even with these incomplete datasets, a crucial part of the historian's role is to organise and filter the available material so that it can be worked into a coherent argument that attempts to answer a series of well-defined questions. One of the key functions that the historian must perform, therefore, is the selection of the data that form the basis of the history that she or he will write. It follows from this that histories are neither as objective nor as value-free as they are often believed to be. Historians determine which questions to ask, which data to use to answer them and which interpretations of those data are most credible. History is, therefore, something that is made in the writing; not a type of knowledge that has a simple objective existence in an unmediated corpus of 'facts'. The historian's function is to produce that writing and, in the process, to transform raw 'facts' into coherent historical narratives. History is, therefore, the end product of what historians do; it is a specialised kind of writing that is organised by a need to explain and interpret 'facts' about the past, but is not reducible to those 'facts' alone. The centrality of this interpretative aspect of history has led some recent historians to invert the order of priorities suggested by Sir George Clark's positivist view of history as comprising a 'hard core of facts' and a 'surrounding pulp of disputable interpretation', and instead to conceive historical study as an essentially interpretative activity more akin to literature-writing than to the rigorous scientific activity that it was understood to be by earlier generations of historians (see Carr 1990: 9–10).

Perhaps more than any other historian, Hayden White exemplifies this tendency. White's conception of history emphasises the constructionist role of the historian, and the multiplicity of interpretations that can be offered for any particular set of 'facts'. History is not, for White, a scientific exercise, but one that is 'essentially a literary, that is to say a fiction-making, operation' (1978: 85). While some have criticised White's approach to history, his recognition of the possibility of taking multiple perspectives in relation to a particular set of facts is helpful for understanding some of the ways in which films and history relate to one another, and we will return to White's ideas later in the book. Before we do this, however, there is another more basic question to ask regarding film's ontological status; what do we mean by film?

It may seem rather nonsensical to ask what a film is, but in terms of its availability for historical study film is a complicated phenomenon. A film has a material existence as a number of reels of celluloid strip containing the images that are projected onto the screen. This is film at its most tangible, and it does have a history: of the changing technologies available for capturing and preserving images; of the development of synchronised sound, colour and widescreen processes, all of which are enregistered on the filmstock itself. But in terms of a movie's social or cultural significance these reels of processed filmstock are only the beginning of the story, and they only really come to life when the reels are removed from their cans and projected onto a screen for an audience to watch. This transitory, ephemeral event, then – the occasion of screening a movie – may be what we mean when we talk about 'a film'. Another possibility lies in the vast amount of documentation created in the process of producing, distributing and marketing the film; yet another in the reviews, interviews and other discussions that accompany the release of a film. The scope of these possibilities means that it is vital for the film historian to limit the scope of the study and clearly define which aspect of a film or group of films is the real subject of the research. Additionally, the relative recency of the entire history of film and cinema provides the historian of film and cinema with access to an abundance of data upon which to draw, usually greatly exceeding anything that historians of earlier periods might hope for. While this increases the availability of the past of film and cinema for historical study, it also increases the burden on the historian to select and filter the available material, and thus increases the extent of the historian's influence on the content of the history that is written.

Because of the complexity of film as a phenomenon and the wealth of material potentially available to the film historian, the term 'film history' has come to signify a disparate range of areas of study rather than a coherent, singular field:

> film is a complex historical phenomenon (an art form, economic institution, technology, cultural product) which, since its inception, has participated in many networks of relationships. In other words, film is an open system. It is not just a set of components forming a whole, but an interrelated set of components that condition and are conditioned by each other. (Allen & Gomery 1985: 16–17)

Even the most cursory examination of the scope of the different areas of activity encompassed by film and cinema reveals the extent of the field, and accordingly film historians have tended to limit its parameters in various different ways. Robert C. Allen and Douglas Gomery divide the field into four major areas, 'aesthetic film history', 'technological film history', 'economic film history' and 'social film history' (1985: 37–8). In a similar vein, David Bordwell and Kristin Thompson acknowledge the existence of a number of different approaches to film history, including biographical history, industrial or economic history, aesthetic history, technological history and social, cultural and/or political history (2003: 5). While schemata of this sort can be useful for conceptualising the field as a whole it is important to recognise that they should not restrict the possibility of undertaking historical work that falls outside these loosely defined areas. Allen and Gomery are clear that the purpose of segmenting the field in this way is not to definitively account for all of film history's diverse facets, but simply to understand that:

> there is no one correct approach to film history, no one 'superhistory' that could be written if only this or that 'correct' perspective were taken and all the 'facts' of film history uncovered. (1985: iv)

Thompson and Bordwell echo this view, arguing that inventories of this sort 'help[s] us understand there is not one history of film but many possible histories, each adopting a different perspective' (2003: 5). Perhaps just as important as this, however, it is vital to recognise that because film is a complex system it is unlikely that any individual example of historical research into film will fall neatly into any of these categories without some overlap with others:

> The artistic effects that can be achieved in the cinema at any given time are in part dependent on the state of film technology. Technological developments are conditioned in many instances by economic factors. Economic decision making occurs within a social context, and so forth. (Allen & Gomery 1985: 17)

In addition to considering the film itself as an artefact that is available for historical scrutiny – a document that reveals something about the time in which it was made and released – it is also important to recognise that films often attempt to take on the role of the historian. If there is merit in Hayden White's suggestion that the work of the historian is not far removed from that of the story teller, then films – particularly those that adhere to principles of realism and verisimilitude – would appear to have the potential to be exemplary histories, promising an unrivalled ability to bring the past to life in a way that written histories cannot. However, there are problems with this simplistic view of the movies. Certainly there is a strong case to be made for acknowledging the important role movies have played in creating and informing common understandings of history. Paul B. Weinstein summarises the issue succinctly: 'think about which has made a greater impression on the mass consciousness, myriad scholarly studies of the Normandy invasion or Steven Spielberg's *Saving Private Ryan*?' (2001). But does the fact that movies represent a more popularly accessible route to narratives about the past mean that we should grant the same status – as a form of valid knowledge about the past – to feature films as to scholarly written histories? One response to this question is to point out that, despite the widespread assumption that these supposedly rigorous, written histories possess greater objectivity than feature films, these histories are also the product of human agency and so are equally susceptible to distortion. For a high profile example of just such a distortion in a written work that claims to be a history we need look no further than the circumstances leading to the conviction and imprisonment, in February 2006, of David Irving for Holocaust denial in his weighty 'historical' tome,

Hitler's War. Although this is an extreme example, it does demonstrate that the political perspective of the historian may be only one of several factors that can lead to a less-than-rigorous treatment of 'factual' data in all histories, whatever form they take. The often tenuous relation between 'hard facts' and the historical narratives that are developed around them may be an effect of what Fredric Jameson has observed about history; that although history itself is not a text or a narrative it is something that is never encountered in unmediated form, and certainly not in a form that is immune to the influence of political ideologies:

> it is inaccessible to us except in textual form and ... our approach to it and to the Real itself necessarily passes through its prior textualisation, its narrativisation in the political unconscious (1989: 35)

Hayden White adopts a similar stance in his consideration of the relationship between 'facts' and the narratives woven around them. He makes a compelling argument that the historian's role is about more than simply recording chronological sequences of events:

> The events must be not only registered within the chronological framework of their original occurrence but *narrated* as well, that is to say, revealed as possessing a structure, an order of meaning, that they do not possess as a mere sequence. (1989: 5; emphasis added)

And the process of providing this 'order of meaning' to the raw facts of history is one that inevitably possesses a political or ideological dimension.

Whether historical discourse is given material form in film or writing it is essential to acknowledge the role played by the historian in the construction of historical knowledge as s/he transforms the fragmented and decontextualised events that we regard as the 'facts' of history into a meaningful narrative form. While both written and filmed histories are, therefore, inevitably susceptible to inaccuracies and outright distortions, it must also be remembered that feature films are created within a matrix of competing pressures – including the desire to be faithful to historical fact, as well as narrative considerations, economic pressures, genre conventions, political and regulatory pressures and so on – that may increase their vulnerability to historical inaccuracies when compared to scholarly written histories. Certainly there has been no shortage of complaints from film scholars about the limits feature films display when asked to provide depictions of historical subjects.[2] Similar complaints about filmmakers' often cavalier disregard for historical detail have also been voiced.[3]

Notwithstanding the fact that these debates about the validity of feature films as a medium for rendering histories still continues, there remains considerable interest among the cinemagoing public in films based on historical subjects, as the recent success of films such as *Good Night, and Good Luck* (2005), *Munich* (2005) and even *Troy* (2004) demonstrates. Indeed a survey conducted in 2000, relating to Americans' uses and understandings of the past, revealed that 81.3% of the sample group had watched movies or television programmes about the past, while only 53.2% had read any books relating to the past (Rosenzweig 2000).[4] The disparity in popular influence between the two forms signals a continuing need to engage seriously with the historical film and to advance our understanding through constructive debate about the problems associated with this mode of history-writing with film. The field of film and cinema history is complicated, and includes the technical, economic, aesthetic and social dimensions of films, the biographies of filmmakers and also the 'history-writing' role of certain films. Considering the extent of this list, it ought to be evident that no single historical study could hope to cover all of these diverse aspects, nor would it necessarily be desirable to attempt to do so. Without wishing to create the impression that some of these approaches are more important than others it is necessary, given the length of this book, to restrict the scope of the remainder of the book to two of the ways that students of film are most likely to encounter some of the issues that the relationship between feature films and history raises.

The chapters that follow, therefore, focus on two distinct approaches to the relationship between films or cinema and history. Chapter 1 looks at the ways in which film scholars have approached the historical reception of films. It examines how film historians attempt to reconstruct the original contexts within which particular movies were produced and first encountered by their viewers, and the impact that historical and cultural contexts have on the meanings that it is possible to make from movies. This chapter is linked to the analysis of Alfred Hitchcock's *Rear Window* (1954) contained in chapter 2. This chapter discusses some of the ways that this well-known movie has been understood by film scholars – particularly those proceeding from the perspective of psychoanalytic film theory – and then demonstrates, in practice, the use of some of the analytical tools employed by reception historians in their efforts to re-historicise films, drawing on a range of contemporary publications in order to illustrate how the film articulates some of the concerns of its historical moment and participates in some of the key discourses of its time. Chapter 3 approaches the relationship between film and history in a very different way, looking at what is often called the 'historical film'. Where the approach of historians of film reception involves understanding films as historical artefacts that register something about the period in which they were created and first released, the 'historical film' is most easily understood as a mode of writing a history of times past. Academic histories may be the most authoritative sources of historical information but they are by no means the only ones, and for the majority of the population it is likely that their main source of exposure to historical 'writing' is not these esoteric tomes but popular historical novels and films that dramatise events of the past in a lively and accessible way. How reliable these popular sources of historical knowledge are, how faithful to the 'facts' of history, and what the implications of this are for the validity of the historical film as a way of understanding history are the questions addressed in this chapter. Chapter 4 then examines this theme further through the use of three case studies. The first looks at the production of David Lean's *Lawrence of Arabia* (1962). In addition to the film itself, this chapter draws on material contained in biographies of the director, published accounts of the life of T. E. Lawrence, the writings of T. E. Lawrence himself and other materials held within the David Lean collection at the British Film Institute, in order to examine the degree to which the film represents a faithful account of the events of Lawrence's life and how far narrative and dramatic considerations have modified the strictly historical dimensions of this film. The second case study looks at the production of *Gangs of New York* (2002); it examines the degree to which the film draws its inspiration from its cinematic heritage and considers what impact this has had on the film's representation of historical events. Finally this chapter examines several recently released films and television movies that take the events of 9/11 as their theme, as well as news coverage of what happened on that day, in order to reveal the processes of mediation that accompany the shift from directly experienced historical events to representations of those events.

1   RECEPTION HISTORIES

First of all, reception studies has as its object researching the
history of the interactions between real readers and texts, actual
spectators and films ... As history, and not philosophy, reception
studies is interested in what has actually occurred in the real world.
(Staiger 1992: 8)

Generally speaking, for many people in many places for a very long
span of film history, the cumulative social experience of habitual
or even occasional moviegoing mattered more than any particular
film they might have seen. (Allen 2006: 60)

The primary aim of this chapter is to explain the development of historical
reception studies, a specialised area of historical film study that focuses
on how films were understood by audiences at particular times (usually
when those movies were first commercially released). At the heart of this
enterprise is a desire to comprehend the meanings attached to films in the
particular contexts within which they were watched and enjoyed by real
viewers. In order to understand why this is such a radically different and
important way of understanding film it is necessary to consider the way
film studies developed as an academic area and how the viewer has been
conceptualised by different approaches to studying film. This chapter will,
therefore, briefly sketch out an account of the development of conceptions

of the viewer or the audience in academic film studies before considering in greater depth the theories, methods and other issues relevant to historical studies of reception.

Film studies and the birth of the film as 'text'

Serious writing on the subject of film has existed almost since the very earliest days of cinema, long before the advent of formal, institutionalised academic interest in the area. The term 'film studies', however, is usually used in a much narrower sense than this, to designate specific approaches to the study of film and a particular institutional setting within which these studies of film have taken place. As an area of academic interest, film studies developed in the late 1960s and early 1970s. Although there are exceptions, it was more often than not the literature departments of universities that provided the most fertile ground for the development of film studies. The combination of this institutional setting and the wider historical context of the first explosion of academic interest in film was particularly significant for shaping the way film was conceived by pioneering film scholars. The timing was important, following the failure of the widespread protests of 1968 – particularly by workers and students in Paris and demonstrations against the Vietnam War in the US – to fatally damage the reign of capitalism. These events provided a particular orientation to the work of these early scholars, as disillusioned left-leaning academics sought out symbolic spaces within culture where either the possibility of challenging capitalist ideologies was preserved or in which the contradictions of those ideologies could be exposed. The institutional setting, within university literature departments, provided a set of ready-made tools – theories and methods imported more or less directly from literary study – that could be used to unpick the workings of film. Film studies developed, then, amid what Leo Braudy and Marshall Cohen have characterised as 'an explosion of new *interpretive* approaches' (1999: xvi; emphasis added).

The crucial term here is 'interpretive', since it clearly signals the degree to which literary approaches shaped the development of film studies in the early 1970s. For these new film scholars the object of study became the film, now regarded as a 'text' and therefore available for analysis using the methods provided by the literary studies background: structuralist linguistics, semiotics, psychoanalytic theory, deconstruction and so on. For Anglophone academics the journal *Screen* became a key locus for the exposition of this brand of film study, delivering such groundbreaking pieces of textual analysis as Jean-Louis Comolli and Jean Narboni's 'John Ford's Young Mr. Lincoln' (1972), Stephen Heath's two-part 'Film and System, Terms of Analysis' (1975a, 1975b) and Laura Mulvey's extraordinarily influential article, 'Visual Pleasure and Narrative Cinema' (1975). Historical approaches to film were not entirely excluded from the pages of *Screen* during this period; for example, the journal published Douglas Gomery's groundbreaking article on the development of sound in the movies in 1976.[1] But while Gomery emphasised in that article the need for a 'revisionist history of the American film industry' (1998: 147), interest in film historiography remained largely 'tangential to [*Screen*'s] preoccupations with film language and with the ideological practices of cinema' (Kuhn & Stacey 1998b: 3). As a result, the majority of film scholars, who regarded their proper focus to be the ideological operations of the film 'text', did not take up Gomery's call.

So far as film studies' understandings of viewers and spectatorship were concerned, this primary interest in the film 'text' had some important implications. Film studies in the early 1970s developed under the influence of two main theoretical strands; Althussarian structuralism and Lacanian psychoanalysis, a combination that film historian Robert C. Allen has disparagingly referred to as 'Lacthusserianism' (1998: 13). Each of these theoretical approaches to film provided a way for scholars to conceptualise the viewer in such a way that it never became necessary to consider real viewers or audiences, or the contexts in which viewing took place. The viewer, whether conceived as a subject in ideology or as one undergoing 'mirror phase' recognition while 'gazing' at the screen was an undifferentiated textual construct that bore no relation to any actual audience member.

As is inevitable in a book of this length, these accounts of Althusser's and Lacan's ideas and their impact on the development of film theory are schematic and over-simplified, as is the explanation of the influence of these ideas on the nascent film studies of the early 1970s. Furthermore, the use of these ideas by film scholars has been subject to numerous critiques over the years, which have led to a dilution and modification of the earliest formulations of Althusserian and Lacanian film scholarship. However, what is important about this stage in the development of the study of films, for my purposes here, is the fact that these approaches allowed film studies to develop with little, if any, interest in members of the movie audience. With its critical eye set firmly on the discursively constructed subject position supposedly inhabited by film viewers, film studies during the 1970s and early 1980s effectively ignored the experiences of real cinema audiences and displayed little interest in the processes through which these real viewers interacted with the film 'text' in order to produce the meanings of films, prompting Philip Corrigan to observe in 1983 that the historical study of film audiences was 'still almost completely undeveloped, even unconsidered' (1983: 24).[2]

It is fair to observe, then, that the viewer/subject as conceived in the early years of film studies was a passive being, constructed by the text and utterly vulnerable to its ideological pressures. Film studies was not alone in thinking about audiences in this way. In the earliest days of mass communication study a model of the relationship between media and audience had been developed that cast the latter in an entirely passive role. This 'effects' or 'hypodermic' model was developed initially in the 1920s, particularly out of the research undertaken in the Payne Fund Studies in the USA. Although supporters of this model can still be found today, it has been widely criticised in film, mass communication and cultural studies, and all of these areas of academic interest in the media have developed more nuanced models of interaction that have shifted the emphasis away from issues about what the media do to audiences and towards an investigation of the way people use the mass media. Whether as a result of the work of 'uses and gratifications' researchers such as Elihu Katz and James Lull or through the research based on Stuart Hall's 'encoding/decoding' model (Hall 1996), undertaken at the Centre for Contemporary Cultural Studies at Birmingham University in the 1970s and 1980s, audiences are now generally seen by media scholars as highly fragmented and differentiated groups likely to produce a wide range of varying meanings from any media 'text'; meanings that are conditioned by factors such as the social identity – race, class, gender and so on – of the viewer and the context in which the 'text' is encountered.

Although both film studies and cultural studies in the 1970s and early 1980s developed quite different (and incompatible) conceptions of media audiences there was surprisingly little dialogue between the two fields of study. Film Studies focused its attention on cinema while Cultural Studies concentrated more on television and, despite some very obvious similarities between both media, the two camps effectively ignored each other until much later on. Shifts in thinking about audiences have taken place within film studies more recently, and now viewers are regarded as much more active and individuated beings. However, the impetus for these shifts has, once again, been provided by changes in the ways that literary theory has conceived readers rather than from any direct engagement between film studies and cultural or media studies.

While film scholars in the 1970s had been busy adapting some of the analytical concepts provided by literary study to the analysis of film, significant shifts had been taking place in literary study itself, as scholars shifted their attention away from the isolated 'text' and towards the instance of reception. In literary studies, as in film studies, it is fair to note that the apparently homogenous term 'reception study' actually covers a number of different theoretical orientations towards reception. These different schools of reception study emanate from different philosophical origins and often provide contradictory accounts of reception but they collectively represent a broad shift in literary study, away from a conception of the literary text as a source of immanent meaning which can be absorbed by a (relatively passive) reader, and towards an understanding of meaning-making as a process that occurs in the interaction between a text and an (active) reader within a particular context. Perhaps the writer whose work best illustrates this shift is Roland Barthes. In his earlier work Barthes exhibits a structuralist's concern with the systems of signification operating in a wide range of different types of cultural text, including food, photography, wrestling matches and cars, as well as literature. Informing this early work is an assumption that meaning resides within the text, where it is produced as a result of the interrelationship between elements of the signifying system, and independently from any individual reader of the text. The text is thus conceived as a perfected, completed entity that doesn't require a reader in order to 'have' a meaning. Barthes' later work, however, is marked by a radical shift away from this structuralist belief in textual unity. By the time he published *S/Z* in 1970, Barthes had moved away from this vision of the text as a coherent, closed structure that orders the reader's experience of it, and instead saw the text as a fragmented collection of units of meaning that provided the reader with no singular, obvious entry route into the text nor any fixed end point. Reaching the end of a novel might be thought to bring finality to the text. But the text always remains available for re-reading in different contexts that can alter its meaning, so that finality is never achieved. For the later Barthes, the text was not to be viewed in isolation, but as an element participating in a network of discourses, within which its meaning is made and remade continuously through the reader's active 'structuration' of the text. According to this view, the meaning of a text is variable and dependent on the reader's own position within the same network of discourses. The process of 'structuration' by the reader is inherently intertextual since that reader 'is already itself a plurality of other texts' (1990: 10); texts, knowledge and experiences that are brought to bear on the 'structuration', or process of meaning-making, of any newly-encountered text.

Looking back to the ideas about textual subjectification proposed by many film scholars in the 1970s, it is easy to see how radical the conception of the reader/subject is in Barthes' later work. While film studies' conception of the process of film viewing demanded a subject who is 'completed' – made whole and coherent in the position constructed for her/him by the text – for Barthes the subject is as open-ended as the text; there is no finality for either since they can both be positioned within multiple contexts that reconstruct both the text and the reader-as-subject.

Barthes was by no means the only literary theorist to embrace a more plural view of textual meaning around this time, nor was this shift limited to those writers who have been associated with post-structuralism. Other literary critics arrived at a similar point via rather different philosophical routes. Two in particular have been considerably influential on the importation of reception study into the study of film: Wolfgang Iser and Hans Robert Jauss.

While holding views that differ greatly in many respects, there are also certain important points of broad agreement between the later work of Barthes and the account of reception and meaning-making offered by Iser. Like Barthes, Iser sees the text as having the potential to yield plural meanings; he views the process of making the meaning of a text as being one that calls upon an active reader who constructs textual meaning by drawing on interior resources gained through the experience of other texts:

> Whatever we have read sinks into our memory and is foreshortened. It may later be evoked again and set against a different background with the result that the reader is enabled to develop hitherto unforeseeable connections ... Thus, the reader, in establishing these inter-relations between past, present and future, actually

causes the text to reveal its potential multiplicity of connections. These connections are the product of the reader's mind working on the raw material of the text, though they are not the text itself. (1974: 278)

While Barthes' later work represents a clear, decisive shift away from earlier conceptions of the text as an entity that has immanent meaning, in favour of one that is a mere element in the textual play of an active reader, the sense of immanent meaning in the text remains to some extent in Iser's work. The reader may be free to re-order the text, but the elements that are available for re-ordering are those supplied by the text: 'the "stars" in a literary text are fixed; the lines that join them are variable' (1974: 282). Although Iser conceives the reader as an active agent who creates meaning in the encounter with the text, the text still does impose some limits on the reader's semiotic activities: the reader cannot make a text mean something that is outside a range of meanings made possible by the elements contained in the text in the first place. Although this is a more limited sense of readerly activity than that suggested by Barthes, it certainly represents a significant shift away from the idea of the reader's subjectification in a position constructed by the text; a position that demands no thought of the reader, demands nothing more than uncritical acceptance of the intended ideological messages of the text.

Both Barthes and Iser, then, propose radically different conceptions of the relationship between texts and their readers than those that dominated film theory in the 1970s. Whether engaged in semiotic 'play' (Barthes) or in 'actualising' the semantic elements provided by the text (Iser), the reader is not seen as the sort of the passive figure suggested by 1970s *Screen* theory. But although the idea that a particular reader has a historically specific existence is implicit in both Barthes' and Iser's accounts, the historical specificity of both the reader and the occasion of an instance of reading is a dimension of the process of meaning-making that is left largely unexamined by both writers.

The work of Hans Robert Jauss attempts to restore a sense of this historical dimension, which he saw as lacking in literary studies at the start of the 1970s when he wrote some of his most influential work. Framing his approach to literary history explicitly as a challenge to more theoretical approaches to meaning production, Jauss noted that the reader had been accorded an 'extremely limited role' (1970: 7) in this area of study. For Jauss, literary theory had developed with restricted views of the historical production of textual meaning and underestimated the importance of the 'triangle of author, work and reading public' in which 'the latter is no passive part, no chain of mere reactions, but even history-making energy' (1970: 8). Jauss's conception of the reader was not of a passive receiver of the text but one who was engaged in an active dialogue with the text. Drawing on some of the insights of genre theory, Jauss developed the concept of the 'horizon of expectation' (1970: 12) that a reader possesses when approaching an unfamiliar text. This includes not only the reader's 'literary expectations but also ... the wider horizon of his experience of life' (1970: 14). Thus the reader's experience of a text in the moment of its reception is conditioned by a complicated matrix of factors that includes the reader's existing knowledge of literature of various genres, and historically specific social factors such as class, race, gender, politics and so on that all contribute to the positioning of the reader. This reader is clearly not, in this formulation, an abstract, ideal reader constructed by the text, but a concrete, socially and historically situated 'real' reader. It is this reader or viewer, in the case of a visual medium like film – a reader that is far removed from the theoretical 'subject' of earlier psychoanalytical and structuralist film studies, who is of interest to scholars of the historical reception of films. With this reader/viewer in mind it is easy to see that the emphasis in studies of historical reception has shifted decisively away from the earlier focus on the film text in isolation to consider the conjunction of the reader, the text and the context in which the encounter occurs. This approach raises some important theoretical and methodological questions, which are considered in the following section of this chapter.

Studying historical reception: issues and methods

If we are interested in studying the reception of a film by real audiences at a particular historical moment then how do we go about actually doing the study, what data will we need, how will we get access to it and what use can we make of it? First, it is important to be clear that although there has been a shift from thinking about the theoretically constructed subject of earlier film studies to considering a historically situated viewer, this 'real' viewer does not – at least in most versions of historical reception studies – necessarily coincide precisely with any particular individual who may have walked into a cinema to watch a movie at a given moment in time.[3] The recollections of these viewers can be accessed by researchers, either through oral histories or documents that viewers may have created (diary or journal entries for example), or through examination of fans' activities and discussions that have become more available for analysis since the advent of the World Wide Web.[4] All of these may be valuable sources of data about the historical reception of a film, where they are available, but they are especially useful when they are used in conjunction with other sources in order to hypothesise the 'conditions of possibility' for understanding a film rather than limiting their use to direct evidence of an individual's response. The aim of historical reception studies – or at least that of the historical materialist approach that I would advocate – should be to examine how viewers might have been able to interpret films in the historical moment of exhibition, taking into account the subject matter and its treatment in the film itself, and the wider social context, the debates and discourses of the time with which those viewers would have been familiar and which would have provided frames of reference within which to make meanings from the material provided by the film. This approach must take account of factors such as the importance of film and cinema within society at the time in question, and also the exhibition context, but its key concern is with establishing 'the identities and interpretative strategies and tactics *brought by spectators to the cinema*' (Staiger 2000: 23; emphasis in original). Janet Staiger helpfully provides a set of working hypotheses that can inform a study of the sort she envisages, and it is worth setting out the first four of these in full:[5]

(i)   immanent meaning in a text is denied;
(ii) 'free readers' do not exist either;
(iii) instead, contexts of social formations and constructed identities of the self in relation to historical conditions explain the interpretative strategies and affective responses of readers. Thus, receptions need to be related to specific historical conditions as events;
(iv) furthermore, because the historical context's discursive formation is contradictory and heterogenous, no reading is unified.

(2000: 162–3)

Several important points arise from these hypotheses. First it is clear that in the model of historical reception studies envisaged by Staiger any sense of meaning being 'contained' in a text has vanished. Equally, however, the reader is not conceived as an unfettered textual libertine, free to make whatever meanings s/he will. Instead both the text and the reader are semiotically constrained by the social setting within which the reception 'event' takes place, since this setting determines the 'conditions of possibility' for making the meaning of a text. In this respect the model proposed by Staiger resembles that suggested by Tzvetan Todorov in which the reader 'constructs the imaginary universe on the basis of his own information (the text, the plausible)' (1990: 46). The invocation of the notion of 'plausibility' here brings into play the socio-historical context in which the reading takes place and the role of that setting in establishing the 'conditions of possibility' for producing meaning. A similar approach to the historical study of film reception is also evident in Tony Bennett's adoption of Pierre Macherey's argument that the study of literature entails

> not just studying the text but perhaps also everything which has been written about it, everything which has been collected on it, become attached to it – like shells on a rock by the seashore forming a whole incrustation. (Cited in Bennett: 1982: 3)

The study of a film's reception involves, then, not just looking at the film but at the whole of the socio-historical setting and at the interplay of discourses within that setting; what Dana Polan has called its 'discursive surround'.[6] However, it is crucial to bear in mind the second important point to emerge from Staiger's hypotheses; that the 'discursive formation' within which a film circulates must be seen as 'contradictory and heterogeneous' (2000: 163). This contrasts with the impression given by many apparently historically informed studies of film, which imply that the culture that surrounds films at a particular time is so unequivocal that particular films, genres or cycles can be treated as emblematic of the general 'mood' or 'tone' of society itself; an approach that Richard Maltby has termed the 'Zeitgeist theory of film as cultural history' (1992: 42). While superficially attractive because of its apparent attentiveness to the historical specificity of the reception of films, the zeitgeist approach ignores the conflicts that inevitably exist in a society at any given time, and presents a misleadingly reductive, idealist and empirically underdetermined vision of social and cultural consensus.[7] Because materialist reception study needs to take account of social tensions and contradictions the method can produce many different, and sometimes contradictory accounts of the reception of a given film at a particular time.[8] The potential for inconsistencies between different accounts of historical reception that this introduces is not, however, problematic for a historical materialist account in the way that it would be for some approaches to film. As Bennett observes – again citing Macherey – the study of 'literary phenomena within social reality' (1982: 3) redefines the text as 'a set of historically specific codes embodied in material notations, that is constantly inscribed within different contexts and caught up in an ever shifting set of relations with other texts, such that it is productive of variable effects and meanings' (1982: 5). Because this reinscription of the text in varying discursive contexts can occur synchronically as well as diachronically, it is possible for conflicting meanings to be made in different encounters with the text in the same historical moment in the same way that it is possible for the meanings of a film to change with the passing of time. And this possibility in no way diminishes the value of the historical materialist approach to film reception: it is not necessary for a reading of a film to be exhaustive in order to be true (see Carroll 1996: 53). All that the possibility of conflicting readings indicates is that films are highly polysemic texts capable of 'speaking' within numerous competing discourses in the same historical moment as well as at different times.

Discourses surrounding the encounter between the film and viewer are crucial, then, to the reception historian's attempt to define a 'horizon of expectation' that could have shaped an audience's interpretation of a film at a given historical moment by circumscribing the 'conditions of possibility' governing the act of interpretation. A key task that the reception historian must perform, therefore, is the identification of sources of data that can provide evidence of what those discourses might have been. While the possibilities for these might appear endless, several common sources have been utilised in a number of studies of historical reception and have proven extremely valuable for providing a sense of the discursive context within which the encounter between films and viewers takes place.

The first of these frequently used resources – and one that has close proximity to the film itself – is the body of pre-release publicity material prepared and circulated by a film's distributors. This might include advertisements in the trade press, official press releases, and press interviews with the film's director and/or stars conducted in order to publicise the film. Some key sources of material of this type that are relatively easily accessible by the film researcher are the pressbooks published by the movie distributors. These are often quite large and contain a range of material that would have been used to publicise a movie prior to its release. While the intended purpose of materials in this class is to generate publicity for the film, these materials also fulfil a secondary function that is of more interest to the academic film researcher; they provide an interpretive frame for the film, indicating what sort of film it is understood to be by its makers and distributors. This reveals something about how the film is intended to be understood by its audiences. By framing a film within the producers' discourses of genre, stardom, realism and quality this type of publicity material tells the audience what kind of film to expect and thus operates in such a way as to constrain the meaning-making activities of audiences. These materials help 'locate a film in its historical moment, identifying the range of meanings offered for it through its exhibition' (Cohan 1997: xvii–xviii). This ability of publicity material to indicate how the studios attempted to position a film around the time of its release can reveal quite dramatic differences between the way a film or group of films was perceived at the time of its initial release and the later examination of the film or films within academic film studies. Perhaps the best example of this can be found in the group of films now understood as belonging to the film noir cycle or genre.

The term 'film noir' is well-known to film students and cineastes alike, and while there are still unresolved debates about numerous aspects of the cycle it is unlikely that many people, at least those who are not well-versed in these arcane exchanges between academic specialists, would dispute that the term designates a specific type of film. These films are defined by the possession of a particular set of aesthetic characteristics (typically for 'classic' film noir, monochrome photography, deep shadows, angular compositions), a concern with particular themes (violent crime, sexual betrayal) and an association with a particular place and period (the USA between the mid-1940s and mid- to late 1950s). However, the term 'film noir' did not come to be widely applied to these films until several years after many of the films now seen as classic examples of the genre were released. Consequently, it is notable that contemporaneous publicity material for the films now understood to belong in the noir canon do not describe the films as 'film noirs' at the time of their release. At the time, the studios and distributors often provided these films with quite different generic identities. Publicity material contained in the pressbook for *The Big Sleep* (1946), for example, is conspicuously lacking in references to those qualities in the film that might be expected in publicity for a film now understood – fairly uncontroversially – to 'belong' to the film noir canon. Instead of an emphasis on crime and violence or the moral ambiguity of its characters, the main promotional strategy for the film on release involved foregrounding the onscreen (and real life) romance of its stars, Humphrey Bogart and Lauren Bacall. Typical posters for the movie were dominated by large images of the two stars accompanied by slogans that highlighted the romantic theme in the film: 'the picture they were born for!', 'this is the love that had to be ... this is the love team you have to see'. Juxtaposing these elements of the film with others that are more consistent with its later re-definition as a film noir,[9] the framing of the film by the publicity material would have powerfully shaped the viewer's 'horizon of expectation' on entering the cinema to see the film and thus the reception experience of viewers seeing the film around the time of its release. During the 1940s and 1950s, a time when no ordinary cinemagoer would have heard of, let alone understood, the term 'film noir', another generic identifier was used to define films now firmly within the noir canon: 'melodrama' (see Neale 2000: 175). And, notwithstanding the fact that it may now be possible to agree that the film possesses the generic attributes expected of a film noir, the earlier definition of the movie as melodrama is also entirely consistent with the blend of romance, drama, action and danger that is foregrounded in the contemporary publicity material for *The Big Sleep*. On the basis of even this small amount of evidence of the way the studio attempted to position the film at the time of its first release it is possible to conclude that the viewer's understanding of *The Big Sleep* in 1946 would probably have been radically different from that of subsequent generations of film buffs and scholars.

A second commonly used source of contextual information relating to the historical reception of movies is contemporary film reviews published in newspapers and magazines. Numerous film reception historians make use of materials of this sort and Janet Thumim, for example, argues that such reviews are an important source of contextual data relating to the reception of movies:

> Critical discussion published at the time of the film's first release remains our only trace of the context in which the film circulated, and is thus a valuable resource provided we keep in mind both its limitations and other contextual factors. (1992: 169)

While I would question Thumim's claim that critical reviews represent the 'only trace' of the original context in which a particular film circulated, they are certainly a unique source of data since they do often represent the only *direct* evidence that is generally available of the outcome of an actual instance of reception of the film.[10] However, the use of published reviews to establish a context for the reception of a film does raise some issues that need to be considered. The major problem with these reviews lies in the fact that the reviewers who write them occupy an extremely privileged position – as opinion leaders – in relation to the films that they review. Additionally, the predominance of white, middle-class men within this privileged group for much of cinema's history means that their views can hardly be seen as representative of the cinema audience as a whole. Furthermore, as Staiger rightly points out, 'the review and scholarly article are genres in themselves; thus their conventions mediate the results' (1992: 89). While these factors point to the need to exercise caution when using film reviews as evidence of reception, none of this means rejecting their use entirely. As a corrective against the possibility that a reviewer's opinions might be the result of personal biases, rather than more widespread societal attitudes, Thumim suggests that the writings of several reviewers should be correlated, paying particular attention to points of agreement and contradiction between them. According to Thumim, these points of consensus and disagreement indicate issues about which, in the case of the former, there was general unanimity, and in the case of the latter, were of 'particular significance to contemporary social struggles' (1992: 169). Thumim also argues that the success of a film at the box office provides a further check against the possibility that the opinions of reviewers might be out of step with those of contemporary society as a whole; 'a film that does particularly well at the box office, whatever reviewers say about it, is clearly one that has some use value to contemporary audiences' (ibid.).[11] While I would not entirely reject these arguments, there are some difficult issues surrounding the use of film reviews that cannot be resolved quite as easily as Thumim suggests. Staiger is more realistic about the limitations of the use of reviews. Although she raises the possibility of supplementing the use of reviews with other sources of data 'such as diaries, letters, small mimeographed newsletters, oral histories etc' (1992: 87), Staiger acknowledges that obtaining such sources is extremely difficult. Ultimately, because of these problems, she is forced to limit the scope of her reception study to small, well defined groups – 'film reviewers and (later) academic scholars' (1992: 89) – rather than the historical cinema audience in general. Despite this limitation, in practice Staiger is able to use film reviews to impressive effect in her analysis of the reception of particular movies, where in conjunction with a wider range of contemporary political, legal and social discourses, they assist Staiger in her project to concretely locate films within their material historical setting.

Although Staiger notes that certain difficulties surround efforts to obtain documents recording ordinary viewers' direct experiences of films and cinemagoing, there are some sources of information of this kind that are more accessible and that have been used by other writers to under-take studies of historical reception. Christine Geraghty's work on British cinema in the 1950s provides an excellent example. She uses a wide range of resources, including the films of the period, letters written by viewers to fan publications such as *Picturegoer* and editorials and articles from the industry publication, *Films and Filming*. But Geraghty goes even further than this, drawing on educational and sociological publications from the period – especially when these were available in popular formats such as 'the famous blue Pelican paperbacks' (2000: xiv) – and on the data collected by Mass Observation, a research organisation that, between the late 1930s and mid-1950s collected data about all aspects of everyday life in Britain. This extraordinarily wide range of data enables Geraghty to go further than merely contextualising individual movies and genres, allow-ing her to provide a fascinatingly rich account of cinemagoing as a social practice during the 1950s.

Both Staiger's and Geraghty's work demonstrate the strength of his-torical reception studies for understanding the meanings attached to films and the experience of cinemagoing in earlier historical times. The method is similar in both cases: using a wide range of contemporary material, including contemporary newspapers, popular magazines and literature, legal, sociological and educational discourses, other films, works of art and even popular songs in order to provide a context or 'horizon of expectation' against which it is possible to reach intelligent, informed conclusion about the meanings that the films, and even the experience of cinemagoing – all too often ignored by traditional 'text'-focused film studies – held for audiences of the time in question.

Geraghty's use of the data collected by Mass Observation represents a significant extension of the range of material available to the reception historian in order to get closer to the experiences of real audience members. The Mass Observation archive, currently housed at the University of Sussex in the UK, provides an extraordinarily rich resource for researchers. Mass Observation started life as a social research project in 1937, with the aim of recording ordinary, everyday life in Britain. It continued in this guise until the early 1950s, when its focus shifted more directly towards consumer behaviour and market research. In the USA the closest equivalent to Mass Observation is found in the research undertaken by organisations more explicitly interested in market research from the outset, such as George Gallup's Audience Research International and Leo Handel's Motion Picture Research Bureau.[12] While the primary materials of these organisations may be less easily accessible than those of Mass Observation, a considerable amount of useful information relating to American movie audiences can be gleaned from Handel's 1950 book, *Hollywood Looks at its Audience*, which distils some of the research conducted by the Motion Picture Research Bureau. Similarly, there have been numerous journal articles published over the years that permit valuable insights into audience attitudes and dispositions in past times.[13] More recently, technological advances have greatly increased the availability of audiences' discourses about movies to researchers. The World Wide Web has a seemingly endless array of topic-specific chatrooms and discussion forums that allow the reception researcher direct access to viewers' discussions about the films they have seen. This facilitates the practice of a sort of 'web ethnography' that allows the researcher to observe and participate in audiences' discussion of films (see Smith 2007). Taken together, these various resources comprise an incredibly rich set of data for the reception researcher and this greatly enhances the ability of reception studies to expose the connections between a film and its contextual surround. Although the vastness of the array of material that could be used to this end might appear to provide a limitless number of potential discursive connections between a film and the surrounding culture, in practice the possibilities tend to be bounded by either the key themes articulated in the film itself or by the particular angle from which the researcher approaches the film. Thus, for example, notwithstanding other possibilities for positioning the film – and given the film's theme and the date of its release, discourses about the Cold War are one obvious possibility – Steven Cohan's analysis of *North by Northwest* (1959), motivated by the writer's concern with representations of gender, and particularly masculinity, considers its relationship to discourses that came to the fore during the 1950s concerning male conformity, domestication and emasculation (1997: 1–33). While these discourses provide a plausible 'horizon of expectation' for the film, and thus enable a materially grounded historical interpretation of the film, this in no way exhausts the possibilities for contextual reading or limits the potential for other historical readings of the movie to be made, taking account of other contemporary discursive frames.

Conclusions

This chapter has outlined the evolution of film studies' understanding of the occasion of reception and the relationship between film 'text' and the viewer, from early accounts of viewer subjection by the text to more recent understandings of reception that conceptualise the viewer as an active producer of textual meaning within the context of a network of discourses that both produce and delimit the possibilities for making the meaning of a film. It has also indicated some of the ways that it is possible to undertake an analysis of the historical reception of films by drawing on a wide range of contemporary contextual materials relating to both individual films themselves and the wider culture within which they were produced and offered to the cinemagoing public. This method enables us to identify the film's affinities with contemporary social and political discourses and its articulation of some of the values and attitudes that were prevalent in its historical moment. While there are limits to this method of reception analysis I would argue that these are outweighed by the strengths of the method. These strengths, derived from the use of empirical data to identify concrete links between films and the surrounding culture, and from the deployment of some of the theoretical concepts provided by literary reception and genre theories – the 'horizon of expectation' and 'conditions of possibility' for making meaning – allow us to make informed and evidentially-based speculations about the meaning-making processes of historical audiences for films. In the following chapter we shall develop the theoretical themes introduced in this chapter further by demonstrating how this method may be used, through an analysis of Alfred Hitchcock's *Rear Window* from the perspective of historical reception.

2   CASE STUDY: (RE)-READING REAR WINDOW

Released in 1954, Alfred Hitchcock's *Rear Window* earned rentals of $5.3m in the year of its release, making it the fifth highest earning film of that year in America (Anon. 1955: 63). The movie was also nominated for Academy Awards in four categories, and for awards from the Directors Guild of America and the Writers Guild of America.[1] For her role in the film, Grace Kelly received a 'Best Actress' award from the New York Film Critics Circle in 1954. Taking all of these indicators into account, it seems fair to conclude that the film was a significant one at the time of its release, having been seen by a relatively large proportion of the cinemagoing public of the day and judged worthy of acclaim by numerous professional organisations within the movie industry. Over the years, *Rear Window* has also proven to be a particularly productive movie for film scholars. Numerous critical writers, approaching the film from a variety of different theoretical perspectives, have produced a large number of interpretations of what must be one of the most debated films of all time. Yet surprisingly, considering how significant the movie was in the year of its release, few scholars have paid much attention to the connections between the film itself and the socio-historical context within which it was produced and first released. This represents something of a missed opportunity for film scholarship, since it is possible to see clear links between the film and some of the key debates of its time, and thus to show how the film participated in important historical discourses that locate it concretely within its historical and social setting. This chapter undertakes a re-reading of *Rear Window* with the aim of revealing some of the connections between the film and its socio-historical setting. There is a two-fold purpose to this exercise. Firstly, that of offering a fresh perspective on this much-discussed movie and, secondly, through the process of undertaking this analysis of the movie, to illustrate the practical use of the approach to the study of historical reception that was discussed in more abstract terms in the previous chapter. I do not claim that the analysis offered here represents the 'last word' on *Rear Window*; that it is the only possible interpretation of the film when approached from the perspective of historical reception studies. Nor am I suggesting that this approach to the analysis of the film supersedes readings of the film that proceed from auteurist, structuralist, psychoanalytic or any other theoretical perspective. All of these approaches have something to offer to further our understanding of this film. However, the gain that reception study provides over these other approaches is that it enables us to locate the film squarely in the social setting of its production and reception. Before embarking on this endeavour, however, this chapter outlines some of the interpretations that other film scholars have offered of *Rear Window* in order to provide a background against which the interpretation offered here can be differentiated.

Visions of Rear Window

One of the earliest and most influential ways of understanding *Rear Window* regards the movie as a metacinematic film; a film about cinema itself. This interpretation of the movie can be traced back to an article published by Jean Douchet in the journal *Cahiers de Cinema* in 1960. Douchet argues that the entire film is a metaphor for cinema itself. The male protagonist, Jeff (James Stewart), is positioned by the film as a voyeuristic spectator who gazes – seeing but unseen – upon the spectacle that unfolds outside across the courtyard; a scene which, Douchet argues, is 'the very projection of himself' (1986: 8). In *Rear Window*, Douchet suggests, 'Hitchcock elaborates his very concept of cinema (that is to say of cinema in cinema)' (1986: 7). Supporting Douchet's analysis of the film, Hitchcock himself seemed to authorise this reading when François Truffaut interviewed him in 1966, when he commented that the film represented the 'possibility of doing a purely cinematic film' (1986: 214).

Combining both an auteurist view of what the film was intended to mean by its creator, and a view that is broadly consistent with psychoanalytic film theory's interest in gendered possession of the look, it is hardly surprising that Douchet's arguments were extremely influential and widely adopted by other film scholars and writers, who have developed this line of argument further over the years. Robert Stam and Roberta Pearson, for example, argued that the most notable feature of the film is 'its status as a brilliant essay on the cinema and on the nature of the cinematic experience' (1986: 193). Stam and Pearson follow Douchet's suggestion that the set used in the film replicates the conditions of film viewing with the film's central male character positioned as spectator among a profusion of cinematic spectacles offered on a number of 'screens' formed by the many windows across the courtyard from his own:

> Jefferies and the apartment complex taken together may be taken to prefigure what has come to be called ... the 'cinematic apparatus', that is, the instrumental base of camera, projector, and screen as well as the spectator as the desiring subject on which the cinematic institution depends for its object and accomplice. (1986: 196)

In another article John Belton advances a version of the same argument, suggesting that 'the set design reproduces the conditions of spectatorship in the conventional movie theater' (1988: 1127) and that the male protagonist represents the spectator 'watching events on a giant screen or series of mini-screens across the way' (ibid). In addition to the similarities between the spatial arrangement of the set and the conventional conditions of movie exhibition, Belton also notes that the spectacles offered to Hitchcock's 'surrogate spectator' represent familiar cinematic genres:

> Miss Torso's window, as screen, recapitulates the subject matter of primitive, pre-1905 peepshows which feature women dressing and/ or undressing and erotic dancing. Miss Lonelyhearts offers us the woman's picture – a melodrama of romantic longing and isolation of the sort found in *Now, Voyager*. The composer's window, barred to symbolise his frustration, reveals ... the essential scenario of a success musical, in which the struggling artist is finally recog-

nised. The couple on the fire escape belong solidly to the world of screwball comedy – that is, until the moment of awful truth when their dog is discovered murdered. And on Thorvald's screen plays a noirish crime film which reworks the murderous love triangles of James M. Cain. (Ibid.)

Not only was this way of conceptualising *Rear Window* as a metacinematic film one of the earliest; it has also been one of the most persistent. In several relatively recent works on the film, various details about the movie are evinced to support this proposition. Introducing a recent anthology of essays about the movie, for example, John Belton describes the set of the film as resembling 'a "montage of attractions", of various windows that display a variety of different "acts"' (2000: 3). Writing in the same volume, Scott Curtis observes that 'immobile and voyeuristic, Jeff is watching several different movies at once – the designers even matched the size of the windows to different screen aspect ratios (2000: 28),[2] while Elise Lemire describes Jeff's position as being similar to the ways that 'cinematic spectators sit confined in their theater seats' and his viewing from the window as being 'just as film spectators view a film in a darkened theater' (2000: 57).

Readings of the movie as an examination of the voyeuristic activities of cinema spectators gained an additional dimension in Laura Mulvey's feminist-psychoanalytic reading of the film in 'Visual Pleasure and Narrative Cinema', which also shifted the emphasis away from the essentially auteurist framework employed by Douchet. The idea that the film is 'about' voyeurism is a productive one for Mulvey, who focuses on this aspect of the film in support of her argument that classical Hollywood cinema organises 'the look' along gendered lines, making the male subject – whether a character in a film or a spectator in the cinema audience – the possessor of the active look while the female figure onscreen can only signify a passive 'to-be-looked-at-ness' (1999: 837). Mulvey argues that *Rear Window* exemplifies the gendered organisation of an eroticised look that exists in Hollywood cinema generally, and which reproduces the different roles of the sexes within patriarchy. On this view of the film's meaning, the crucial moment in the movie comes when Lisa (Grace Kelly) crosses the courtyard and enters Thorvald's (Raymond Burr) apartment to investigate the suspected murder of Mrs Thorvald. Of this scene Mulvey argues that

His girlfriend Lisa had been of little sexual interest to him ... so long as she remained on the spectator side. When she crosses the barrier between his room and the block opposite, their relationship is re-born erotically. (1999: 842)

Thus, for Mulvey, as for those other critics who focus more directly on the purely metacinematic aspects of the film, *Rear Window* remains fundamentally a film about looking, and although Mulvey's argument did open up new avenues for debate about the film, these hardly diverted academic discussion of the movie very far from its well-trodden path. Thus, although Tania Modleski's (1988) critique of the Mulveyan position in her analysis of the film reaches a very different conclusion from that of Mulvey, Modleski's reading of the movie still centres on the issue of possession of the active gaze and so remains rooted in the tradition of criticism about the film that is concerned with its articulation of the gendered dynamics of scopophilia, or pleasure in looking. For all that has been written and said by academics about *Rear Window*, there is little evidence of much interest in the film's status as a document of its time, an artefact that might reveal something about the important issues and debates, the concerns and anxieties, the attitudes and values of the historico-cultural formation in which it was produced and originally circulated.

More recently, film scholarship has begun to call attention to more historically oriented questions about *Rear Window*'s ability to articulate something about the wider social context of the USA in the early to mid-1950s. Armond White, for example, suggests that the movie represents 'Hitchcock's post-World War II uncovering of average American loneliness, deception, mundanity and horror' and that the film's 'elements of spying and snooping probe the postwar experience of American rejuvenation and political tumult' (2000: 123, 124). Another writer, Scott Curtis (2000), draws on contemporary publicity materials and reviews in his account of the making of the film while a third, Elise Lemire, attempts to redress the inattentiveness of both Mulvey's and Modleski's readings to the 'historical specificity of gender dynamics' (2000: 64) by attempting to locate the film within the distinctive social currents encountered in the USA during the early 1950s. Ostensibly, Lemire's reading endeavours to connect the film to 'the specific conditions and dynamics of 1950s culture in the United States' (ibid.), particularly discourses concerning domesticity, the growth of suburbia and the now frequently invoked 'crisis' that beset masculinity during that period. Drawing on cultural histories of the period and on contemporary popular literature such as Sloan Wilson's *The Man in the Grey Flannel Suit* (1955) and Robert Lindner's *Must We Conform?* (1955), Lemire makes a convincing argument for seeing the film as a contribution to debates about masculine conformity and the emasculating effect of the drive toward domesticity that engaged the American public during the 1950s.

Film scholarship of the kind undertaken by Lemire represents a significant step forward from the decontextualised auteurist and psychoanalytic accounts of earlier writers, and has a much greater likelihood of producing the kind of analysis of the film that is capable of indicating something about the range of interpretations that would have been available to the movie's original audiences. The scope of Lemire's analysis may be limited by the narrow range of extra-filmic materials that she utilises, but the method she employs demonstrates the gains that can be made by the scholar who draws on as wide a range of contemporary materials as is available in order to develop an understanding of what the film was likely to have meant to contemporary viewers.

Janet Staiger embarks on a similar project in her reading of the film, attempting to balance an interpretation of the film text with a concern to identify some of the 'possible reading strategies of the mid-1950s' (1992: 82). Noting that her attempt to produce a historical materialist account of the film's reception is necessarily constrained by the limitations of the available contextual materials and that, as a consequence of these constraints, her 'reading public' consists only of contemporary film reviewers and later scholars of film, Staiger identifies four discourses that were employed in contemporary reviews of *Rear Window*; psychoanalysis, authorship, genre and the social. The importance of the first two of these to film scholars should be readily apparent from the earlier parts of this chapter. It is worth noting, however, that Staiger's research reveals, among other things, that the use of these two discourses as framing devices for *Rear Window* is not entirely an imposition of later film theory, but is also apparent in some contemporary reviews of the film. As Staiger notes, psychoanalysis was an extremely influential discourse during the 1950s, being widely popularised in American culture after the mid-1940s, and so it is hardly surprising that this discourse would inform reviews of a film made and released in the early 1950s that is manifestly interested in issues of voyeurism and scopophilia. So far as the auteurist discourse identified by Staiger is concerned, this is hardly surprising either since, at the time of the film's release in 1954, Hitchcock had a well-established reputation as a director, and his reputation would certainly have been highly relevant to the film's reception at that time. Robert Kapsis has argued that 'from the beginning of his directorial career ... Hitchcock used publicity to promote himself, his films, and the idea of directorial preeminence and authority' (1992: 16). This reputation undoubtedly forms an important part of the 'horizon of expectation' against which the work would have been evaluated (1992: 11). Once again, then, it is unsurprising that references to Hitchcock's reputation as a film auteur with a well-defined oeuvre should be used by contemporary film reviewers to discuss the position of *Rear Window* within his body of work. So far as genre – the third discourse detected by Staiger in contemporary reviews of the film – is concerned, discussion of a newly-released film in relation to genre and its generic predecessors is unremarkable in a film review; genre is another important factor in establishing a horizon of expectation for any newly-released movie.

Staiger's intention is not to provide an exhaustive analysis of the reception of *Rear Window* and it would be unfair to criticise her analysis for not considering a wider range of contemporary discourses in order to provide a greater sense of the film's interconnection with important social discourses of the time. What Staiger's reading does provide, however, is a strong sense of the contrast between the historical materialist approach that she advocates and other analytical methods. It is evident, however, that a materialist contextual analysis of *Rear Window* can be taken further than the accounts offered by both Staiger and Lemire, and is capable of producing an understanding of the film that radically departs from the trajectory defined by the conventional psychoanalytic/auteurist understandings of the film as one that is primarily concerned with voyeurism.

The remainder of this chapter demonstrates the presence in *Rear Window* of traces of a number of social discourses that had come to prominence in the USA by the early 1950s. Like Staiger, I do not claim that what follows represents an exhaustive analysis. Rather, this should be seen as extending her approach and as representing a radical break with psychoanalytic and auteurist modes of film criticism. It is hoped that the analysis offered here represents a productive starting point for identifying new possibilities for understanding *Rear Window* historically.

Rear Window

Rear Window begins with one of the few scenes in the film that is not organised primarily according to the visual perspective of its male protagonist,
L. B. Jefferies (James Stewart) or Jeff as he is called throughout the film. As the film's titles roll, three blinds covering the windows of Jeff's apartment are pulled up one-by-one to reveal the courtyard across which Jeff will observe the lives of his neighbours. After the final blind is retracted the director's credit appears briefly, then vanishes and the camera begins to move toward the window. A cut to a position outside the window then allows the camera to perform one of the film's signature shots, 'an elegant, almost 360° panoramic camera sweep' (Sharff 2000: 14) around the courtyard before returning through Jeff's window and pausing briefly on a close up of Jeff's sweating brow as he sleeps in front of the open window. The opportunity that this survey of the film's set gives the viewer to understand the spatial relations between different parts of the set is crucial to the establishment of Jeff's central position in the visual economy of the film, the position conventionally occupied by the cinema spectator. Thus the shot is an important element in the establishment of the cinematic metaphor that pervades the film and that so many film scholars have perceived as key to understanding the film. Following a line of argument first suggested by Stam and Pearson (1986: 197), Michel Chion considers the significance of the relationship between the panoramic sweep of the camera and the brief pause on Jeff's sleeping head at the end of the pan, arguing that the effect of the sequence as a whole is to establish the status of the courtyard, and the action that will take place in it (including the murder of Mrs Thorvald that also takes place as Jeff sleeps), as a projection of Jeff's dreams or fantasies (2000: 111). Following this brief pause on Jeff while he sleeps there is a cut away to a brief shot of a thermometer in Jeff's apartment before the camera begins another survey of life in the apartments across the courtyard – a pan to the songwriter's apartment to the right of Jeff's window; a cut to the couple sleeping on the fire escape of the building opposite Jeff's apartment; a pan that pauses at Miss Torso's window and passes that of the sculptress before returning to the sleeping figure of Jeff. This time the camera does not remain on his head, but pans down his body to reveal the plaster cast that encases Jeff

'Here lie the broken bones of L. B. Jefferies': damaged masculinity in *Rear Window*

from his waist to the toes of his left leg and bears the words 'here lie the broken bones of L. B. Jefferies'. The camera pulls back to reveal that Jeff sleeps in a wheelchair, then pans across the room to show the smashed camera and photograph of a racing car crashing that explain Jeff's condition, together with various other pieces of photographic equipment, some photographs and finally a framed negative image of Lisa (Grace Kelly) and the positive image of the same photograph on the cover of a magazine. The shot then fades to black. The opening sequence lasts only 2 minutes and 22 seconds but even in this brief scene the voyeuristic tone of the movie, considered by so many academic critics to be its defining feature, is clearly established.

This sense of voyeurism is so insistently foregrounded that it is quite easy to overlook one of the most significant aspects of this scene so far as its participation in contemporary social discourses is concerned. When the camera pans from the thermometer to the songwriter's window we see the songwriter shaving in his studio and hear the first diegetic dialogue in the film, an announcement on his radio:

'Men, are you over forty? When you wake up in the morning do you feel tired and run down? Do you have that listless feeling?'

Although some other scholars who have written about *Rear Window* have made a point of noting this announcement, the psychoanalytic perspective that governs so many academic readings of the film conditions their interpretations of its relevance. Bertolini, for example, notices this line of diegetic sound (2002: 235), but connects the announcer's words to the dream state imputed to Jeff, and so interprets this line in a way that is consistent with the claim that events in the film represent the wish fulfilment of the central male consciousness that is presumed to structure the film's representational strategy. However, the announcement also performs a referential function that connects the film to some of the key social discourses of the time and thus would have provided another 'horizon of expectation' for audiences in the early 1950s.

Before tracing the discursive connections suggested by the radio announcement, it is worth considering the operation of the announcement itself in relation to the film's viewer using some of the concepts supplied by film studies. The voice on the radio is diegetic; it speaks to characters in the film and forms part of the soundscape of the courtyard that is such an important part of the film's realism. But it also addresses the spectator in the cinema audience. 'Men': The first word spoken in the film breaks through the jaunty extra-diegetic music that runs through the opening titles and first scene, fracturing the film's seamless aural continuity up to this point. This break signals a transition in the film, a shift from the predominantly visual address of the opening titles and the first camera sweep around the courtyard, which the extra-diegetic music helps to identify as a part of the process of establishing the cinematic metaphor of the film. With this diegetic radio announcement the film shifts into a narrative mode that requires the spectator's complicity in the film's realist representational mode; that demands submission to its verisimilitude. 'Men': surely an almost perfect example of an Althusserian 'hailing', a call to occupy a subject position constructed by the film; a 'hey, you there!' which causes the spectator to turn and recognise himself as the subject addressed. 'Men', this film is about you. The words that follow immediately, 'are you over forty?', modify the hailing and narrow down the terms of the address. The film calls the spectator/subject as a man but is primarily concerned with middle-aged men. Finally, before the songwriter retunes the radio, the announcer asks, 'When you wake up in the morning do you feel tired and run down? Do you have that listless feeling?' These words establish the problematic to be investigated in *Rear Window*.

Lemire's analysis of the film correctly identifies the much-vaunted 1950s 'crisis of masculinity' as being central in *Rear Window*. But Lemire fails to pursue some of the key discourses of the period relating to masculinity and the male body; discourses that substantially contributed to the idea that masculinity was in crisis. This line spoken by the radio announcer signals a rather concrete crisis of masculinity that came to the fore of the public consciousness in the USA during the late 1940s and early 1950s: a crisis precipitated by the revelation of the relative fragility of the male body and its propensity to premature decrepitude. This is a key element in the film and also in social discourses about men which had widespread currency at the time. And, if the radio announcement does not signal this concern clearly enough, it is indexed again when the camera dwells briefly on the words inscribed on Jeff's plaster cast: 'Here lie the broken bones of L. B. Jefferies'. This concern of the film with the fragility of the male body registers a discourse which emerged into US popular culture around the middle of the 1940s and which had come to particular prominence in 1953, the year before *Rear Window* was released.

Several recent newspaper articles – 'Who's a pretty boy?; Breakthroughs, tips and trends' (Naish 2005: 3), 'Official: men are the frailer sex' (Lezard 2006: 22); both popularised accounts of academic research – might suggest that the idea that male bodies may be weaker and more vulnerable to illness than those of women is a fairly recent discovery. However, this discourse about the relative fragility of the male has a much longer history. In April 1944 the magazine *Science Digest* published an article, 'The Weaker Sex Is – Male' (Anon. 1944a), a condensed version of another article that had appeared originally in the journal *Hygeia*. These two articles drew on 'extensive data' which, they argued, pointed to a need 'to revise many of our notions regarding the so-called weaker sex' (1944a: 1). The article sought to expose the fallacy of the traditional belief that men were the stronger of the sexes, suggesting that this belief was nothing more than a myth and that it lacked any empirical basis:

> The evidence suggests that our traditional attitude toward woman is in large measure merely a social custom passed along from antiquity – not founded on any real physical frailty of the female. (Ibid.)

Continuing along the same line of argument, the article cited the longer lifespan of women, the higher mortality rate for infant males, the higher male suicide rate and the greater susceptibility of men to debilitating illnesses as compelling reasons for concluding that, 'In the Darwin [sic] concept of survival of the fittest, it is difficult to escape the conclusion that females are endowed with greater biologic vigor' (1944a: 2).

These articles in *Science Digest* and *Hygeia* were not alone in raising the issue of male fragility. An article published in the *Readers Digest* in April 1945 – 'How Much Do You Know About Men?' – (condensed from yet another article that first appeared in *Woman's Home Companion* in the same year) followed a similar line of argument. Arguing against the 'common-sense' suggestion that male bodies are constructed 'more perfectly and efficiently than women's' (1945: 23) the article noted that

> Males come into the world with many more malformations and organic weaknesses. Their bodies are more likely to get out of order, and chemically they don't function as efficiently. (Ibid.)

Furthermore, the article also argued that men's bodies age more rapidly than those of women:

> Under average conditions a man's body deteriorates more rapidly so that he is biologically older than a woman of the same age. He is less resistant to most diseases, and with other hazards his remaining lifespan is shorter than the woman's. (Ibid.)

In a similar vein, an article in *Time* magazine noted that 'woman is also the stronger sex ... she is a much more efficient organism for survival' (Anon. 1944b: 55).

These assorted articles articulated a very concrete 'crisis of masculinity' that came to prominence in scientific discourse (and its popularised versions) toward the end of World War Two, and continued to circulate in American culture for several years after. These discourses, and others that dealt with various different aspects of maleness and masculinity, ensured that interest in the 'problem' of masculinity remained a focal concern of American society from the late 1940s and through the 1950s. Although World War Two was an important factor in the crystallisation of these anxieties, they persisted long after the war ended and, with the passing of time, gained additional support from numerous diverse directions.

In 1948 the publication of *Sexual Behavior in the Human Male* by Alfred W. Kinsey and his colleagues further challenged traditional assumptions about American male normalcy, with its (at the time) shocking revelations about, for example, the number of men who admitted to having homosexual experience. Kinsey's second inquiry into sexuality was published in 1953 as *Sexual Behavior in the Human Female*. Like the male volume, this became an almost instant bestseller and so the revelations of these two reports rapidly became part of the common currency of American popular culture during the early 1950s. As bestsellers, Kinsey's two reports became particularly influential in setting the agenda and defining the terms in which human sexuality was discussed in America at the time. For this reason Kinsey's findings are especially relevant for understanding how *Rear Window* articulates an anxiety about men (a 'crisis of masculinity') precipitated by the dissolution of myths of male physical strength and virility. Kinsey's discovery that women's sexual desire peaked later in life than men's and then remained at a fairly constant level – in contrast to the steady decline of male sexual desire from early adulthood – is particularly relevant. Kinsey's data suggested that sexual desire (and stamina) peaked during men's late teens or early twenties and then entered a fairly rapid decline. In contrast, Kinsey's findings suggested that women's sexual desire increased steadily through their twenties, reaching its peak in the mid-thirties, and thereafter remained at a fairly constant level. This revelation was sensational and controversial, upsetting conventional wisdom that cast mature men as potent and virile beings and women as more sexually passive. However, this reconceptualisation of male and female sexualities also fits extremely well with other contemporary discourses relating to the propensity of the male body to decrepitude at an earlier age than women, and with the construction of Jeff's character in *Rear Window*.

In the year of *Rear Window*'s initial release, James Stewart was 46 years old and while the film does not indicate the age of his character, there is no reason to suppose that Jeff's age is intended to be greatly different from that of the actor. Jeff, a middle-aged man, once a man-of-action – as we know from the references in the film to his career as a photojournalist – now finds himself incapacitated and incapable of doing anything other than passively gaze out of his window. In attempting to understand how these discourses about the fragility of the male body and its physical decline in middle age may have provided a 'horizon of expectation' for viewers in the mid-1950s, it is instructive to make some comparisons between the film and another released just over a year later, *Picnic* (1955), starring William Holden. Although Holden was ten years younger than James Stewart, in the roles they play in these two films, the age difference between the two actors does not seem to have any bearing on the very different visions of masculinity they project in the films; both are constructed as mature men. There are, however, radical differences in the way the physicality of their characters is represented. In his analysis of *Picnic*, Steven Cohan makes a rather throwaway comment about the contrast between the sight of Holden's muscular chest and arms in that movie, and the chest of James Stewart, when it is briefly exposed in *Rear Window* when Jeff rises after receiving a massage from Stella (Thelma Ritter). However, this is a contrast that deserves more careful consideration than Cohan allows, since it signals the importance in *Rear Window* of the declining physical power of the male body. As Cohan argues of Holden's role in *Picnic*, the exposure of his body places him in a position that, according to some feminist approaches to film, is the position of spectacle. This is a position conventionally occupied by the figure of woman in classical Hollywood films and the placing of

The male body in decline: *Rear Window*

Holden's body in this position feminises him, according to Cohan (1997: 170–1). However, as Cohan also points out, contemporary fan discourses relating to some of the era's most popular male stars also made use of similar images of Hollywood 'beefcake' (1997: 164–5), and while these images were unquestionably there 'to-be-looked-at', at another level what they offered to those who looked were aspirational visions of a masculine ideal. It would be difficult to say the same of the bared torso of James Stewart in *Rear Window*. Where the bare-chested Holden in *Picnic* moves fluidly and exhibits his strength and well-toned muscularity through physical labour, Stewart rises awkwardly from the bed because his movement is inhibited by the plaster cast that envelops much of his lower body. And the torso that is briefly exposed by this movement possesses none of the muscularity of Holden's chest. Stewart's muscles lack definition and his skin hangs loosely on his body providing an image of a middle-aged male body that has long ago passed its physical peak. 2.1). The physical representation of Jeff is thus consistent with the way that the film registers contemporary social discourses about masculinity, and especially about middle-aged men. *Rear Window* goes further than merely registering these discourses, however; it also foregrounds the disjunction between the 'reality' of the middle-aged male body, as it was conceived in these contemporary discourses, and the mythical ideal of masculinity that dominated Hollywood's representations of men and that perpetuated the traditional image of men as possessors of superior physical strength.

To understand this aspect of *Rear Window* it is necessary to resurrect the idea of the film as a metaphor for cinema itself, with Jefferies positioned as spectator watching the action on a number of 'screens' across the courtyard. The key 'screen' (the 'main attraction') is Thorvald's window. What is presented on that screen is an image of masculine physical power that is consistent with the idealised images of masculinity promoted by contemporary films such as *Picnic*, but which stands in stark contrast to the newly-discovered 'reality' of the fragile male body in middle age, as it is constructed by the wider range of contemporary social discourses identified earlier and which is represented by Jefferies' character in the movie. *Rear Window* thus constructs an opposition between the material reality of male embodiedness and the idealised, ideologically constructed masculinity that retains the aura of physical strength and power traditionally

The myth of masculine power: *Rear Window*

associated with the male figure. This overarching dichotomy is articulated through several related oppositions linked to the characters of Jefferies and Thorvald:

Jefferies		*Thorvald*
broken	:	whole
fragile	:	virile
weak	:	strong
feminised	:	masculine

Crucially, the film makes no distinction between the two men on the basis of age. Although Raymond Burr was nine years younger than James Stewart, the film itself does nothing to suggest that there is any great disparity between the ages of the two characters that they play. Indeed with his portly physique framed by the window through which he is most often seen in the film and with his hair coloured grey, Burr appears to be rather older than he would a few years later when he started to appear in the television series, *Perry Mason* (1957–66). Both Jefferies and Thorvald represent men in middle age: the former, a socially-referential construction of middle-aged manhood, conditioned by contemporary popularised versions of medical and scientific discourse, while the latter remains true to an ideologically maintained belief in the superior physicality of men. At this point the reading for *Rear Window* suggested here becomes more consistent with the reading of the film as a metaphor for cinema suggested by numerous other writers. Thorvald does represent a ideal of masculinity for Jefferies, the movie spectator, not because he acts out in the diegesis what Jefferies can only fantasise about – ridding himself of the 'burden' of a wife, and the commitment and loss of male autonomy that go with marriage – but because he is physically everything that Jefferies is not, but has been told that he should be by countless idealised images of masculinity and discourses about what it means to be a man. *Rear Window* registers, then, both the ideological imperative to maintain an image of male physical power upon which the political and economic advantages of men in society were built, and the more progressive contemporary discourses that threatened to expose this image of male superiority as a mere fantasy.

Although the main vehicle for the articulation of these discourses concerning male fragility is Jeff's character, there are other ways these are registered in *Rear Window*. The revelation of a disparity between the sexual drives of men and women, in Kinsey's research, provides the basis for one of the recurring jokes in the film. Most scholars who have written about *Rear Window* have understood the newlywed couple that occupies another of the apartments facing into the courtyard as simply another projection of Jeff's anxieties about marriage. But the couple also illustrates – through the recurring joke that is incorporated into their appearances in the film – the excess of female sexual energy over that of the male; an excess that, as Kinsey's 1953 report on female sexuality indicates, became increasingly pronounced as men and women advance in age.

In a scene close to the start of the film Jeff watches the activities that take place through a window just to the left of his own, as a newlywed couple is shown moving into their first apartment together. After the building manager gives the husband the keys and brings their luggage into the room he departs, leaving the couple alone. They begin to kiss, but the husband casts a look at the apartment door, breaks away from the kiss and moves to open the door. The couple leave the apartment briefly before returning, this time with the husband carrying the bride over the threshold. They start to kiss again, but the wife (still dressed in all white, although not

The arrival of the newlyweds in *Rear Window*

her bridal gown) says something inaudible and looks toward the window. The husband then discreetly draws the blinds leaving the viewer to imagine that the scene that continues out of view, behind the blind, progresses rapidly from kissing to the sexual consummation of the marriage. The viewer's attention is directed to the newlyweds' window on several further occasions throughout the film. Two of these are particularly instructive. On each of these occasions the husband, wearing a vest and pyjama trousers, pulls up the blinds. The husband leans through the window showing clear signs of physical exhaustion. Almost immediately the wife's voice calls out his name, summoning him back into the apartment and into the marital bed to satisfy her demands. Although these scenes featuring the newlyweds are obviously played for comic effect, the way *Rear Window* constructs these minor characters – the husband who is quickly exhausted by the wife's seemingly insatiable sexual demands – also registers the finding of Kinsey's 1953 report, that female sexual energy exceeds that of the male, particularly as age advances.

Rear Window is contradictory, however, and while it does register Kinsey's findings through this secondary detail, the film also tries to reframe the mismatch between the sexual drives of men and women in terms that would have been more reassuring to 1950s America's patriarchal culture, through its construction of another of the film's minor characters, Miss

Lonelyhearts. Throughout the film we witness the increasing desperation of Miss Lonelyhearts, a mature woman who yearns to find a male partner. In one scene Miss Lonelyhearts sets the dinner table in her apartment – across the courtyard from Jefferies' window – for two people, as if expecting male company. However, the companion turns out to be imaginary, and she sits down alone, while continuing to hold a conversation with her fantasy man. Later in the movie, when she does finally succeed in enticing a male companion back to her apartment, the man is much younger than Miss Lonelyhearts, a fact sufficiently noteworthy to attract a comment from Jefferies: 'he's kinda young isn't he'. Like the window of the newlyweds' apartment, the blinds are soon drawn over Miss Lonelyhearts' window, but this time the action within remains visible through the slats of the venetian blinds. The young man's sexual eagerness is evident, but although Kinsey's findings suggest that they should be well matched in terms of sexual desire, the young man's clumsy mauling is not what Miss Lonelyhearts desires. She slaps the man's face and ejects him from her apartment. So although, on the one hand, *Rear Window* registers some of the most sensational findings of Kinsey's report on female sexuality through the brief scenes that foreground the newlyweds, it also re-moulds Kinsey's revelations about the active sexuality of women into a more traditional and patriarchally reassuring narrative that insists that what women desire is love and romance, rather than the pure physicality of sex. In this way *Rear Window* attempts to restore more traditional ideas about male and female sexuality – that women desire sex only within the context of loving relationships while men possess a more profligate desire for sex, driven by physical pleasure rather than emotional intimacy.

This effort to restore traditional normative conceptions of the sexual behaviour of men and women is also apparent in the film's ending. At the end of the film the camera completes another sweep around the courtyard. In the musician's apartment we see the musician together with Miss Lonelyhearts. Although her flirtatious demeanour and her words about the musician's newly recorded song – 'I can't tell you what this music has meant to me' – hint at the possibility of a romance developing between the two characters, there is a clear contrast between this scene and Miss Lonelyhearts' earlier encounter with the younger man: the characters remain some distance apart in the later scene, signalling that this relationship is framed within the ideology of romantic love rather than discourses relating to purely physical sexual desire. The musician is another middle-

Miss Lonelyhearts accepts a kiss from her fantasy man in *Rear Window*

aged man and the film's implication is that he is a better match for the mature woman, Miss Lonelyhearts, than a younger man, notwithstanding the reported mismatch between their sexual desires. In this respect the film conforms to the very traditional moral view of women's sexuality contained by an ideology of romance; one that would deny women's possession of a sexuality based on the physical pleasures of sex, just as this latter understanding of female sexuality was beginning to gain recognition following the publication of Kinsey's 1953 report.

Conclusions

The analysis of *Rear Window* that is proposed in this chapter should be seen as a complement to existing scholarship about the movie. In this reading the film may still be understood as a metaphor for cinema, as numerous earlier film scholars have suggested. Indeed, such an understanding is essential for appreciating how the film constructs the series of binary oppositions between Jefferies and Thorvald. These oppositions articulate the disjunction between the ideal masculinities promoted through popular cultural forms and the contemporary scientific discourses that had begun to conceive the material reality of embodied maleness as a physically fragile state that did not, in reality, correspond to these idealised visions of masculinity. This disjunction became the subject of widely circulating social discourses in the years immediately before the making and original release of *Rear Window* and it is not surprising that their influence is perceptible in the film. A key difference between the analysis offered here and much of the existing scholarship is that the cinematic metaphor in the film does not refer to the cinema as an abstract construct of film theory, but a cinema – and a regime of representational practices associated with the cinema – grounded in the material reality of the historical moment at which the film was made and offered to the viewing public. *Rear Window*'s representational strategies are not formed solely by a set of abstract aesthetic conventions that mould the film into an inherently meaningful text. Rather, it is necessary to recognise the fact that the cinematic conventions of meaning-making inscribed within the film 'text' operate within a wider cultural context from which the film draws intertextual elements into its representational repertoire, elements that would have been readily recognisable to contemporary viewers and that would have been operationalised by them as a 'horizon of expectation' for the film. In the type of historical analysis offered here, recognition of the contextual location of the film is at the heart of the analysis.

Of course different viewers will always have slightly different 'horizons of expectation' – even at the same historical moment – and so will operationalise different intertextual elements in their processes of making the meaning of a particular film. The use of widely known contemporary discourses – rather than obscure, esoteric ones – to provide the contextual frame for a film can help to minimise the effect of this. However, it cannot eliminate it completely and this historical approach to film analysis will never fully be able to account for the ways that differences in the positions inhabited by social individuals – and here class, race, gender and sexuality are likely to be key factors in the production of a range of divergent readings – alter the way a film is understood by its audiences, even those viewing the film at precisely the same time.

Approaching a film through a materialist historical framework does not, then, produce an exhaustive, comprehensive account of how that film was understood by its viewers. It does, however, have an advantage over less historically oriented approaches by making it possible to gain an empirically-grounded understanding of the potential for making the film's meaning by audiences at a particular time. Far from foreclosing on the possibilities for viewers' meaning-making activities, this approach to the historical reception of films constantly opens up new prospects for examining the range of different understandings available to viewers: in what (probably very different) ways would *Rear Window* have been understood in the early 1950s by women? How would African-Americans have understood it? How would working-class viewers have interpreted the film? Using the methods of reception studies it becomes possible to start to consider these important questions.

3   HISTORY WRITTEN WITH LIGHTNING

> 'If it is right for historians to write history, then by similar and unan-
> swerable reasons it is right for us to tell the truth of the historic past
> in motion pictures.'
>
> D. W. Griffith (1915)[1]

The idea that film might be used as a way of presenting history has been
in existence for a considerable time, almost since the very earliest days of
moving pictures. There may be a rather obvious, common-sense appeal to
the idea that the past can be brought to life in moving images in a way that
it cannot in serious written work. Surely film, with its exceptional capacity
for verisimilitude, can show us history as it was, while the dry prose of
an academic text can only tell us about it in a way that makes it seem
more distant, less alive. In practice, however, the attempt to render history
alive on screen raises numerous difficult questions. Consequently the idea
of using film as a way of 'doing' history has been controversial, and the
subject of frequently heated debates between scholars of history. Some of
these debates have also entered into more widespread public ideas about
what history is.

A discussion that took place in the 'Notes and Queries' section of the
Guardian newspaper in 2004 provides a good illustration. The discussion
focused on what the public perceives as the key issue at stake in relation
to historical films: 'Why do Hollywood directors find it virtually impossi-

ble to make a reasonably accurate historical film?'[2] The question drew a number of responses. One reader quoted Alfred Hitchcock: 'It is not the responsibility, nor the interest, of an artist to document historical reality' (see Anon. 2004: 17). Another reader suggested that the reason was pure, cynical commercialism; a case of giving audiences what they want to see regardless of the degree to which this necessitated a distortion of histori-cal facts. This reader cited *The Birth of a Nation* (1915) as an example of a movie that demonstrates that the 'problem' of Hollywood's 'dishonest' approach to history is almost as old as cinema itself' (ibid.). Yet another reader echoed Hitchcock's view that Hollywood is primarily in the business of entertainment, not history, and also suggested that the idea of historical 'accuracy' is itself a problematic concept (ibid.).

Notwithstanding the easy disclaimer of any responsibility towards his-tory found in the Hitchcock quotation above, the fact that filmmakers do produce films based (however loosely) on historical events and persons makes it necessary for film scholars to give more serious consideration to some of the difficult epistemological questions that are presented by his-torical narratives produced primarily as a form of entertainment. This need is particularly compelling in the case of cinema, since feature films have long been, and still remain, an extremely popular form of entertainment, and thus a key way in which members of the general public engage with history. The epigraph to this chapter signals one of the reasons why this is so important. Hitchcock may have been happy to deny any responsibil-ity towards historiography in his filmmaking, but other filmmakers have positively embraced the challenge of rendering past events alive on the screen and have implicitly, and often explicitly, claimed that the matchless verisimilitude of film makes it a superior medium with which to illustrate the events of the past. The value-laden wording of Griffith's comment – that historians merely 'write history' while filmmakers are able to 'tell the truth of the historic past' – represents an unambiguous assertion of film's superiority over the written word in the task of bringing the past alive for the audiences of the present. However, as well as the ambivalence towards that task demonstrated by Hitchcock in the above quotation (and surely shared by many other filmmakers), numerous other factors – industrial, commercial, aesthetic, generic and so on – govern the work of filmmakers and shape the results of their endeavours in ways that are inconsistent with the high ideal of historical veracity to which Griffith laid claim. In this and the following chapter we shall examine some of the key issues and debates that have arisen as a result of filmmakers' attempts to present history on the screen. While chapter 4 will examine these issues through a series of case studies that examine some of the practices involved in 'historical' filmmaking, this chapter takes a rather more abstract, theoretical approach to the debates that have arisen in both film studies and in the study of history, concerning film's aptness for articulating a valid form of historical knowledge. As will become clear, this is a more complicated area of debate than a simple concern over accuracy.

What is history today?: empirical history and language

While the discussion of Hollywood's apparent lack of concern for historical 'accuracy' in the *Guardian* (presumably) took place between non-historians, working with common-sense and intuitive notions of what history is, the points raised by these correspondents bear a striking resemblance to some of those that have dominated the debate among professional academic historians and film scholars about film's suitability for developing an understanding of the past. But, as this chapter aims to demonstrate, the invocation of sanctified notions of 'accuracy' or 'truthfulness', as if these are unproblematic qualities possessed by 'serious' academic works of history but lacking in all other forms of historical representation, is at best an anachronistic approach and at worst a positively misleading simplification of some rather complicated issues relating to the epistemological status of the traditional type of written academic history.

History, as most non-historians (at least those educated within a western, Anglophone context) will understand it — the history based on important dates, events, persons and an underlying sense of economic, political, technological and social progress through decades and centuries past and on into the present — is itself the product of a particular confluence of historical forces. This kind of empirical, 'scientific' history that most of us will have been taught in school came into being during the nineteenth century under the influence of some of the prevailing social and intellectual trends of the time, particularly the industrial revolution and the Enlightenment. These trends, especially the latter, promoted the spread of scientific thought and methods into a wide range of different fields of intellectual activity that had often previously been shaped by radically different epistemological principles. Although I will refer to the style of historical thinking associated with this type of history as 'traditional', it is important to remember that it is a tradition that has a history of its own – one that is not all that long – and that its emergence and development have been the result of particular material historical conditions. Although it is often tempting to see this approach as natural or organic, in fact it is nothing of the sort. Although often presented as being neutral and objective – as having an almost mimetic relationship to those events in the past with which it concerns itself or, in other words, mirroring the past while only minimally (if at all) distorting the events it depicts – this approach constructs rather than reveals history. This approach to history has been challenged from various positions, particularly in recent years, yet it nevertheless continues to exert considerable influence over the way that many non-historians understand history. From this position of pedagogical authority it has attempted to fend off challenges from other ways of representing the past, including film. In recent years, however, this approach to history has been challenged on a number of fronts, by 'new historicism' on the one hand and perhaps more significantly by the broader postmodern critique of Enlightenment epistemology, which has paved the way for a new breed of postmodern historians whose understandings of what counts as history are more pluralistic and inclusive than those of the more traditional type of historian.[3] The postmodern critique of the traditional, empirical school of historiography emerged initially outside the academic discipline of history, as part of a more extensive critique of epistemology and knowledge production that originated within the disciplines of philosophy, linguistics and literary studies. It is worth briefly examining the development of postmodern thought in these areas in order to understand the theoretical foundations upon which the postmodern critique of traditional empirical approaches to history is built.

Before the early years of the twentieth century, the dominant theories of linguistic meaning had held that there was a mimetic relationship between language and material objects in the world: that things have an objective existence in the world and are merely described by language. However, a succession of theoretical paradigms that came to prominence in linguistics and literary theory after the early years of the twentieth century – structuralism, post-structuralism and postmodernism – challenged this view by insisting that rather than neutrally mirroring entities that have an objective existence, language actually constitutes them as objects, endowing them with a meaning that comes from the system of language itself rather than any innate property of the object. The earliest of these paradigms, structuralism, still held that a relationship – albeit an arbitrary and conventional one – existed between the linguistic sign and the material object (the referent). Post-structuralist and postmodern theorists have, however, progressively moved further away from that position, insisting that the relationship between signifier and referent plays no part in the process of linguistic meaning-making; it is the relationships between signs and other signs that enables meaning to be produced in language.

This shift in thinking has had significant implications for the traditional, empirical approach to history, which is founded on a belief that historical 'facts' have ascertainable objective meanings in themselves. To frame this in linguistic terms, these historical 'facts' are referents to which the sign (writing about history) refers, and when traditional historians write their histories they take their task to be the revelation of the inherent meaning of these referents, not the construction of the past within a system of representation that is far from neutral.

Postmodern critics would argue against this traditionalist position, insisting that even the most rigorous of these 'scientific' histories is unable to provide direct, unmediated access to the historical period or event under examination. According to the postmodern critique, scholarly written histories must themselves be viewed as representations of the past – the fragmentary and essentially ambiguous raw material of historical data transformed into a coherent story that brings the past to life – rather than as a neutral mirror that reflects the past without altering or distorting it in any way. Thus the practice of writing history is inevitably enmeshed in its own system of representation. As such, the endeavour to produce rigorous scientific histories is fundamentally flawed, since it is impossible to put the reader in the position of experiencing the past directly. 'Scientific', empirical history is thus founded on a denial of the figurative and rhetorical qualities of historical writing. One historian who has embraced the postmodern critique of traditional history, Keith Jenkins, argues that

> when it is abundantly clear that history as a genre of literature is
> necessarily the product of rhetorical figures and devices; when its
> realism is unavoidably the realism of the figure, then what defines

academic history and shapes it as an empirical, epistemologically
striving discipline is precisely its reluctance to face these facts.
Academic history thus constitutes itself in denial. (2004: 367–8)

For Jenkins the profession of the academic historian is built upon a refusal
to acknowledge and confront the creative uses made of source materials by
professional historians; a denial that is enshrined in historical method in
order to maintain an image of the profession as scientific and objective. This
image does not coincide with the reality of academic practices of historical
writing, which are in fact every bit as reliant on rhetorical and figurative
language to construct 'history' as any ostensibly less rigorous form of historical 'writing'. Oliver Daddow takes this argument even further, pointing
out that not only is the act of writing history a process of constructing a narrative about the past, but very often the documents from which historians
obtain their 'facts' are themselves the result of efforts by contemporaneous
chroniclers of historical events to provide a coherent narrative account of
those events. For now it is enough to note that even the sources of 'original'
information upon which histories are based are already somewhat removed
from the actual events to which they relate and, as a result, these traces of
the past are liable to contain a marked 'fictive element' of their own (2004:
426). The importance of this point will become very clear in the following
chapter, which analyses the relationship between news coverage of 9/11
and the history of the events of that day.

Acknowledging the problem raised by this facet of the process of history-writing is not to deny that facts exist or that historical events take place.
Rather it is to recognise that the written histories based on those facts
are not the same thing as the facts themselves. These histories actually
have more in common with other types of historical representation – literary and other representational forms that possess an explicitly fictive
element, such as the historical novel and the historical feature film – than
many traditional historical scholars, with their scientific aspirations, would
willingly admit:

Events undoubtedly occur: the Declaration of Independence was
signed on 4 July, 1776, yesterday it rained, Napoleon was short, I
had a nice lunch. But to be construed as 'history' such facts must
be selected and arranged on some sort of plan, made to resolve

some sort of question which can only be asked subjectively and from a position of hindsight. Thus all history writing requires a fictive or imaginary representation of the past. (Slotkin 2005: 222)

Richard Slotkin, an academic historian who has also achieved success as a writer of historical fiction, is well placed to observe the interrelationship between the two forms of historical activity, as well as the merits and limitations of each form of historical writing. Slotkin argues that both genres of historical writing – History (with a capital 'H') and historical fiction – have something valuable to offer when it comes to advancing our knowledge about the past. The historical fiction, he argues, provides an outlet for the historian's understandings of the period or event in question that cannot be proven according to the rigorous evidential standards demanded by the academic discipline. The choice a historian must often make, according to Slotkin, is between 'telling the whole story as he or she has come to understand it; or only what can be proved, with evidence and argument' (2005: 223). This is an important point about the writing of history, which highlights the presence of a significant creative element in historical writing. And while Slotkin's solution to the academic historian's dilemma of how far this creative component should find expression in written histories is to impose a separation between his more rigorous work and his more creative work, it is important to note that he does not thereby create an epistemological hierarchy between the two genres of writing, in which one mode of historical writing is held out as superior to the other. The rigorous, scholarly historical study expresses what can be 'proved' while the historical fiction expresses what the historian understands about the period or event in question but cannot prove. However, neither is an outright falsification of history and both constitute important forms of knowledge about the past. Slotkin's conception of historical writing extends the categories of writing available without creating a binary dualism between the two forms. Indeed, he perceives them as being complementary rather than oppositional.

Slotkin's acknowledgement that there is a fictive element even in rigorous academic histories displaces this mode of historical writing from the privileged position often claimed for it by more traditional historians and re-positions it alongside other forms of 'writing' that also claim to tell us something about the past. Re-conceived in this way, it becomes clear that scientific history is not a form of transcendental 'truth', but a product of the material, historical conditions that have facilitated its development. As such, this mode of historical writing has more in common with other forms of historical knowledge than its practitioners would often care to acknowledge. One of these other forms, myth, predates the 'scientific' approach to history that developed in modernity and provides us with a useful way of understanding history as a form of writing, and film as a mode for writing history.

Most common-sense understandings of the term 'myth' conceive it as a form of story telling that is essentially untrue. However, within the frequently fantastic stories that are associated with myth there is often a significant amount of factual content. As Rebecca Collins points out, 'to claim that myth is a false version of some event, there must be some significant commonalities between the accurate account and the false version, otherwise there would be no reason to suppose that they referred to the same event' (2003: 343). While myth, therefore, possesses none of the rigour expected of academic histories, there are elements in myths, as in historical fiction, that must correspond to the same facts upon which 'scientific' histories of the events in question are based. Rather than seeing myths as outright falsifications or distortions of historical truth, then, Collins argues that myth should be conceived as the 'other' of 'scientific' history. This 'other' should not be viewed as the antithesis of 'scientific' historical truth – or, to put it another way, an outright distortion or fabrication of events, persons and so on – but as an alternative form of historical narrative, one that contains some 'significance' about the past that is not to be found in the 'scientific' type of history (2003: 345). In suggesting that 'significance' is a crucial factor in the production of historical knowledge, Collins echoes Slotkin's argument that historical fiction enables the expression of knowledge about the past that cannot be proved rigorously. Collins' invocation of 'significance' also raises another important point relating to all forms of historical story telling, whether of the 'scientific' type of history or another, such as myth or historical fiction, namely that for every historical story there must be an anticipated readership in the present for whom the story must be capable of having meaning. In other words any historical story is inevitably the product of two historical moments; that from which the historical data on which the narrative is based are drawn, and that within which the historical narrative is written and read. And it is for this readership of the historical work in the present that the story must have meaning or 'significance'. Collins argues that:

> the past is not something that is fixed and apprehended for its own sake. Rather the past is studied only to the extent that it is unified with an interest of the present life. The study of history is bound up with the present not by choice but rather by epistemological necessity. (2003: 346)

That our historical knowledge about the past is founded on the concerns of the present is a fact that the notable American historian, Richard Hofstadter, was happy to admit; 'I still write history out of my engagement with the present' (quoted in Brown 2006: 97). Thus rooted at least as much in the present in which it is written as the past that it takes as its refer-ent, history – be it 'scientific', mythical or the explicit historical fiction – always bears the impression of the prevailing attitudes and values of the culture at the time of its writing.[4] History 'must have a face and the face it bears will in part be determined by the presuppositions belonging to the historical time in which the account was written' (Collins 2003: 350).[5] Recognising, then, that the historian will always to some extent play the role of story teller – selecting from a fragmented and disordered array of facts from the past, deciding which to foreground and ordering them into a narrative organisation that will be meaningful for the contemporary reader – Collins argues that there is a dissolution of the boundaries that sepa-rate myth and history and a convergence between both forms of historical narrative (2003: 358); both have their basis in the same facts and both are produced through the creative activity of human agents who have a material existence within a particular configuration of social, political and economic forces. Consequently, Collins also suggests that there has been a progressive movement away from the idea that history can accurately and 'truthfully' (in the absolute sense) represent the past. Accompanying this shift is a growth in the recognition that history is inevitably 'contempo-rary, engaged, competitive and political' (2003: 359), that it is

> constituted rather than found. It is about *creating meaning* from the scattered, contradictory and meaningless debris we find around us. (Wilcox 2005: 344–5; emphasis added)

This sense of history as construct shaped in part by present values and attitudes (political, ideological and social) – a sense that is evident in the revised conception of historiography demanded by postmodern theories – is well illustrated by considering the reception of, and attitudes towards D. W. Griffith's *The Birth of a Nation* upon its release in 1915.

The Birth of a Nation and the social situatedness of history

On 18 February 1915 D. W. Griffith's *The Birth of a Nation* – at the time still showing in a few cinemas (prior to its official premiere) under its original title, *The Clansman* – was screened in the East Room of the White House for an audience consisting of President Woodrow Wilson, his family and other senior government officials. The film apparently impressed the President who, according to numerous accounts, declared that it was like 'writing history with lightning'.[6] While there may be some doubt about whether the President did actually utter the remark now frequently attributed to him, it is likely that Wilson, a prominent scholar of history before his presidency, did generally agree with the account of the civil war and reconstruction periods that are presented in *The Birth of a Nation*: the film is broadly consistent with Wilson's own thesis about the development of the sense of nationhood in America, contained in his *History of the American People,* first published in 1901. Indeed, Wilson's book is quoted in several of the intertitles in the movie and was cited by Rabbi Charles Fleisher, during his testimony at a public hearing relating to the exhibition of the film in Boston in 1915, to demonstrate that *The Birth of a Nation*, 'while not precisely accurate historically, is generally correct' (quoted in Lennig 2004: 132). This view of the film, as one that presents a broadly true account of the civil war and reconstruction periods, was probably quite widely held at the time of the film's release. As Arthur Lennig notes, 'almost everyone, except for a very few citizens (not all of them black), believed that it was a fair representation of historical facts' (2004: 123). However, other views of the film's debateable historical virtues did exist at the time of its release. Rabbi Stephen Wise, for example, described the movie as an 'indescribably foul and loathsome libel on a race of human beings' (2004: 125). Similarly the *New York Globe* reconsidered its earlier favourable review of the film and reversed its earlier opinion, criticising the movie for its distortion of history (ibid.). According to Lennig, however, dissenting views such as those of Rabbi Wise and the *Globe* were less widely held around the time of the film's release than is now commonly believed. *The Birth of a Nation*

> was generally extolled for being an accurate and stirring dramatisation of America's past and was almost universally praised by film reviewers, editorial writers, historians, clergymen, politicians, union leaders, socialists, and the public at large. (2004: 137)

'To most viewers' argues Lennig, 'it was no more than "teaching history with lightning"' (ibid.). There were, of course, protests against the movie by the National Association for the Advancement of Colored People (NAACP) and its supporters on the grounds that it presented an unfavourable image of African-Americans. But despite this, and the fact that the understanding of the film as generally historically truthful was in large part the result of the careful manipulation of contemporary public perceptions of the movie through the use of publicity by both Griffith and Thomas Dixon (the author of the novel on which the film is based), the vision of the civil war and reconstruction period presented by *The Birth of a Nation* was one that a majority of Americans at the time found easy to accept. The reason why the movie's vision of the era was so widely accepted was because it accorded, in general terms, with popular American views of the period at the time of the film's release: '*The Birth of a Nation* drew mainly favorable reviews and large crowds, both because of Griffith's cinematic innovations and *because he effectively dramatised the prevailing views about the Civil War era*' (Browne & Kreiser 2003: 59; emphasis added). At the time of the film's release, popular views of the earlier period were dominated by a vision of the civil war and reconstruction as a ' "tragic era" characterised by black excesses and white suffering' (ibid.). This was the view that had been developed and promoted by the historian William Dunning and his followers (the so-called Dunning School). The 'history' that *The Birth of a Nation* recounted may have been no more than a presentation of Dunning's views of the reconstruction, supplemented with what Everett Carter terms the 'Plantation Illusion'; a nostalgic, romantic vision of the antebellum South as a 'golden age' in which 'feudal agrarianism provided the good life for wealthy, leisured, kindly, aristocratic owner and loyal, happy obedient slave' (1998: 12). However difficult it may be for viewers today to accept that the vision of the South presented by *The Birth of a Nation* represents anything resembling a reasonably truthful historical account, for audiences at the time of the film's release this 'profoundly perverted history' was one that 'Americans found easy to absorb' (Litwack 1996: 138). According to Leon F. Litwack's account of the film's reception, the American public was very willing to accept the version of history presented in Griffith's film for several reasons pertaining to the state of race relations and racial attitudes in the USA in the early part of the twentieth century:

> The Birth of a Nation appeared during the most repressive and vio-
> lent period in the history of race relations in the South. Between
> 1890 and 1915, in the face of racial tensions heightened by growing
> evidence of black independence and assertiveness (the New Negro),
> whites acted on the prevailing orthodoxy to ensure their absolute
> supremacy and the permanent political, economic, and social sub-
> ordination of the black population ... At the same time, the findings
> of 'science' and the learned professions and the dissemination of
> dehumanising caricatures reinforced and comforted whites in their
> racial beliefs and practices. This was the America that The Birth of a
> Nation explained, vindicated and celebrated. (Ibid.)

Several important general points about the presentation of history on film can be found in the debates that The Birth of a Nation has provoked over the years. First, the general willingness of American audiences at the time of the film's initial release to accept the vision of the civil war and reconstruction presented by Griffith's film demonstrates the important role played by the contemporary social and political context in determining what kind of history it is possible to write at any particular time. It is quite possible that Woodrow Wilson did regard the film as history written in lightning, because that version of 'history' was not only entirely consistent with his own published views about the role played by the Ku Klux Klan in establishing order in the postbellum South and in forging of a sense of national unity after the reconstruction, but also with the dominant historical, and public, understanding (the myth) of that period at the time of the film's release. The lesson here seems to be that where a film is broadly consistent with the historical orthodoxy of the moment it will raise few objections from the establishment historians of the time or from large parts of the general public. In 1915, The Birth of a Nation was consistent with what

Roland Barthes has termed the 'doxa' of the time – its 'common-sense', taken-for-granted assumptions – and for this reason it was easy for people to accept its validity as a historical account.

Changing times, changing values

As the case of *The Birth of a Nation* demonstrates, historical knowledge is not a stable entity which, once established, can thereafter be regarded as settled for all time. Revisionist historians later forced a reconsideration of the view of the reconstruction era offered by Dunning and his followers, and later political shifts in American society, particularly in the wake of the Civil Rights movement in the 1960s – which led to the development of more progressive and enlightened attitudes towards race – also forced a reappraisal of the vision of 'history' offered by *The Birth of a Nation*. All histories, then, whether on film or in scholarly books and articles are subject to challenges and to later revision. This is clearly the case when new evidence becomes available. More significant, however, are the revisions of 'history' that can also arise without substantial new evidence, but in response to changing social values and attitudes that require that the existing evidence be re-interpreted in a way that is more consistent with those new values. This point is particularly important when it comes to evaluating the suitability of film as a medium for rendering history since it underscores the fact that history itself is far less stable and monolithic than those who would unfavourably compare history on film with scholarly written histories would contend. Rather than an inviolable, scientific 'truth' about past events, history is an unstable and provisional construct that is as much the result of the cultural politics of the present in which the particular history is written as it is the product of the raw data about the past upon which it is based. And if the very concept of history is itself unstable, and histories of particular events are liable to be rewritten in light of changing social values, then there is no particular reason why the mode of historical 'writing' cannot change too, in response to technological developments that make available new media for rendering the past alive in the present. This sense of transition between different ways of writing history, and also the link between these periodic transitions and the development of new technological means for making history available to the public, is very clear in Robert Rosenstone's observation that 'the challenge of film to history, of the visual culture to the written culture, may be like the challenge of written history to the oral tradition' (1988: 14). It would be misleading, however, to view the relationship between these different ways of telling the story of past events as one of obsolescence and supersession. The coming of literacy did not eradicate the oral history nor has film displaced the scholarly written history although it has opened a new dialogue between these different modes that have the potential for 'writing' history.[7]

Filmed history

As argued in the preceding section of this chapter, postmodern re-considerations of the nature of historiography have shifted the epistemological status of the 'scientific' type of history sufficiently from its previous position of dominance to allow other ways of telling history to stand alongside the more traditional type of written academic history as equally apt, but different, ways of producing knowledge about the past. However, even a cursory look at how these alternative approaches achieve the aim of informing us about the past reveals that these different ways of 'writing' history achieve their ends through very different techniques and provide very different types of knowledge about the past. And while postmodernism may have challenged the 'scientific' approach to history sufficiently to allow other ways of 'doing' history to stake their claims to being valid ways of knowing about the past, it is very clear that the different media through which historical knowledge is created and communicated are far from equal so far as the extent of their influence is concerned:

> Today, the chief source of historical knowledge for the majority of the population – outside of the much-despised textbook – must surely be the visual media … it is not farfetched to foresee a time … when written history will be a kind of esoteric pursuit and when historians will be viewed as the priests of a mysterious religion, commentators on sacred texts and performers of rituals for a populace little interested in their meaning. (Rosenstone 1988: 1174–5)

According to Rosenstone, history fulfils a larger social purpose than merely providing a description of the past: it provides a 'web of connections to the past that holds a culture together' (1988: 1175). With this function in mind, movies – with their greater popularity than academic histories and thus their ability to reach large numbers of people – begin to appear more convincing as a way of providing the general population (who probably rarely, if ever, read 'serious' academic histories) with access to this 'web of connections'. Despite the grip that film has on the popular imagination, however, debate still rages about its limitations as a way of 'doing' history. In one corner are historians who regard film as superior to the written word when it comes to rendering the past as a complex whole. R. J. Raack, for example, argues that film is better suited than writing to capturing the chaotic, complex and contradictory qualities of the social world than conventional written histories which are, as Rosenstone puts it, 'too linear and too narrow in focus to render the fullness of the complex, multi-dimensional world in which humans live' (1988: 1176). In the opposing corner, other historians dispute the possibility that film can provide a meaningful historical account of past events. Ian Jarvie, for example, argues that the historian's function is not simply to provide a descriptive narrative of past events – such as might just as well be articulated in the form of a movie as a book – but to enter into debate with other historians about 'what exactly did happen, why it happened and what would be an adequate account of its significance' (Jarvie 1978: 378). As Rosenstone observes, the contradiction between historians like Raack and those who would align themselves with Jarvie's position arises from the fact that both schools of thought conceive history in rather different ways. For Raack, history is a way of gaining affective access to 'the experience of people's lives in other times and places' (ibid.). For Jarvie, history is a more rigorous, scientific exercise in which evidence about past events is systematically weighed, evaluated and debated by specialists in the field. There is a further dimension to the opposition between these two positions, which is implicit in Rosenstone's account of the debate but which is perhaps worth spelling out, and that is that each understanding of history is inextricably linked to a particular vision of the identity of the human participant in historical discourse. While Raack envisions a history that is accessible to all, Jarvie's conception of history requires an expert, well-versed in the technical and methodological intricacies of evidentiary evaluation and possessing the confidence that this expertise provides to participate in debate with other experts. Raack's view represents a populist conception of what history is, and is unsurprisingly more open to acceptance of the use of film as a mode of historical 'writing'. Jarvie, on the other hand, locates the practice of history firmly within the academy (or at least among sufficiently well-educated intellectuals possessing the necessary cultural capital), and its own distinctive traditions and modes of writing.

Rosenstone takes issue with several assumptions that underpin Jarvie's pessimistic assessment of film's potential as a mode of historical 'writing'. In response to Jarvie's claim that film carries a 'poor information load' (ibid.) Rosenstone points out that there is, in fact, an 'enormously rich load of data' held within the visual image (1988: 1177). Each individual image is much richer in quotidian detail and far exceeds in its complexity the ability of the written word to render an equally intricate image of the same scene: even a single shot in a movie possesses such a wealth of detail that to attempt to capture a similar level of detail in a written description of the same scene would be an almost endless task. Adopting a similar stance, Hayden White rightly points out that 'the historical evidence produced by our epoch is often as much visual as it is oral and written in nature' (1988: 1193) and, as such, demands a different set of skills of the historian from those appropriate for the analysis of written documents. White argues that history on film should not be seen as a supplement or complement to written history, but as an entirely different kind of historical discourse with its own distinctive representational practices, its own syntax and grammar (1988: 1193–4). He argues that, for any historical period in which visual data such as photographs exist, history rendered on film is likely to be more accurate than any written history since such imagistic evidence 'provides a basis for a reproduction of the scenes and atmosphere of past events much more accurate than any derived from verbal testimony alone' (1988: 1194). White, therefore, rejects the suggestion that the scholarly historical monograph necessarily possesses a superior claim to accuracy at all. Taking these arguments into consideration, it becomes apparent that Jarvie's denial of the appropriateness of film for 'writing' history on the basis of its unsuitability for rendering detail signals that his conception of history is founded on some deeply embedded assumptions about what details actually matter when it comes to understanding the past. While films may be rich in detail about the everyday lives of people in past times, such as costumes of the period and reconstructions of historical locations, there may be rather less emphasis on the close analysis of major political, social, economic and military events, their causes and consequences that, for a historian like Jarvie, constitutes the very stuff of history. So while films may be rather better than traditional written academic histories at conveying certain kinds of information about the past, they are less suitable for providing the political, economic and social commentary that is the currency of academic histories. It follows from this that how film's aptness as a medium for 'writing' history is evaluated depends on the relative value attached to different aspects of the past – Jarvie apparently regards the quotidian details that film is particularly well-suited to conveying as less important than analysis of the exceptional or notable events that 'make' history in the more traditional understanding of the term.

Since they effectively conceive history in fundamentally different ways; one as a democratic means of accessing a general – though not necessarily rigorously accurate – understanding of life in past times, the other as a specialised and rigorous empirical enterprise open to only a small constituency of experts – the contradictions between these two positions are not easily reconciled. Although his own position is probably closer to that of Raack than Jarvie, Rosenstone sensibly avoids having to decide between the two by arguing for a wider conception of history, which permits the coexistence of an array of different types of historical 'writing' that includes both the historical film and the scholarly written history. As Rosenstone points out, even among the more 'serious' written histories, there is no standard format for the work: 'on many historical topics, one can find short and long works, for the amount of detail used in a historical argument partakes of the arbitrary or is at least dependent on the aims of one's project' (1988: 1178–9); but this variability does no damage to the credibility of the work. Similarly, while film may not possess the same analytical density as the written word, and so cannot provide the same sort of history as the academic monograph, its limitations in this area are counterbalanced by its far greater ability to 'directly render the look and feel of all sorts of historical particulars and situations' (1988: 1179). And, since much of the evidence on which historical 'writing' is based (whether actually in print or on film) is itself visual, the role of the historical filmmaker is not one of translation from written or verbal material into visual form, with the concomitant concern this inevitably raises that something important might have been 'lost' in the process of translation. The historical filmmakers' endeavour is that of recreating the original scene visually, a task that is greatly aided by the availability of visual traces of the original time and place. According to White, rather than regarding film as a translation of a (superior) written discourse, it is necessary to acknowledge the differently constructed narrativity of both filmed and written histories (1988: 1195) and the tendency of both forms to employ 'shorthand' representational strategies such as stylisation and stereotyping. These techniques inevitably distort the accurate reproduction of original details within the historical narrative to some degree, but do so in the interest of achieving a broad historical verisimilitude within the work as a whole (1988: 1199). The issues raised by historical films represent a challenge to more traditional approaches to the subject; a challenge that opens up new possibilities for understanding history, in a similar way to that in which the written word transformed an earlier oral history tradition. In challenging the written word's dominion over history, historical films both reflect the increasing importance of the visual media as a mode for communicating knowledge through the twentieth century and up to the present, and offer an opportunity for extending the horizons of our historical understanding so as to include the quotidian and the affective dimensions of life in times past – what did it look like? what did it feel like to live in those times? – in addition to the recounting and analysis of exceptional events, which remains a key element of our understanding of the past.

Conclusions

This chapter has taken an abstract, theoretical look at some of the difficult questions raised by the claim that film represents a valid way of 'doing' history. The following chapter will take a different approach to these questions, by attempting to give some of the issues raised by this discussion a more concrete basis through a series of case studies of particular films that can in some way lay claim to the label 'historical'. The claim that the historical film represents a valid way of knowing the past may remain a contentious one for some time in certain quarters. However, one recent development may signal a growing acceptance among historians of the film's aptness for this task, or at least a willingness to take the question seriously. In the May 2006 edition of *Perspectives*, the monthly newsletter of the American Historical Association, Robert A. Schneider, editor of the *American Historical Review*, announced a change in that journal's policy in relation to film reviews. While the journal had in the past carried brief individual film reviews, the editorial indicated that these would in future be replaced with 'extended review essays on films of historical interest' (2006). Explaining the reasons for the change in policy, Schneider acknowledged that one of the problems with the journal's past treatment of film arose from the fact that 'our reviewers have usually been historians with little training or expertise in film studies and often with little interest in the medium other than as moviegoers'. Unsurprisingly, noted Schneider, 'the dominant approach of reviewers has been to assess the historical accuracy of a film, paying little attention to the specificity of film as a language or mode of representation'. While this still falls somewhat short of recognising that written history is also a 'language or mode of representation', it nevertheless signals a significant shift in the attitudes of academic historians towards film. This shift concedes that there is a need for historians to take film seriously as a way of 'doing' history and to start to open up a dialogue between written and filmed histories that moves beyond the simple dismissal of film's validity as a way of writing history because of its failure to adhere to the same practices as are expected of a written scholarly history. For academic historians, then, if not for those readers of the *Guardian* discussed at the start of this chapter, it seems that the debate about film as a way of rendering history may finally be moving beyond the rather misleading question of 'accuracy' and towards a more serious engagement with the opportunities and problems that attend the attempt to use film as a way of understanding the past.

Adherence to the facts

4　PUTTING HISTORY ON FILM

The previous chapter examined some of the debates that have been generated by the attempts to establish film as a valid and instructive way of portraying real events from the past. It argued that the field of historical study has in recent years been opened up by the intervention of postmodern theorists in such a way as to include an expanded range of forms of representation within the definition of the 'historical', including the historical film. As the argument goes, since the scholarly written history possesses the same textuality as other ways of representing history and since all ways of representing history have some basis in 'facts' about the past, there is no reason for privileging one mode of historical representation over others. They are all valid (but different) ways of representing the past. Buried within the superficially seductive logic of this argument, however, are several assumptions that should not simply be taken for granted. Historical films may indeed have some basis in fact, but how closely do filmmakers actually adhere to these facts in practice? In addition to these questions concerning film's adherence to facts, what impact does the unique combination of historical discourse and specifically filmic discourses have on the ability of filmmakers to remain close to the facts of history upon which a film is ostensibly based – to what extent may the historical narrative in a film be shaped by aesthetic considerations; by genre, drama, stars, spectacle?

These questions will be addressed in this chapter through the use of a number of case studies that examine how the ideal of using film to bring the past to life has been realised in practice. The films discussed in this chapter have been chosen because they provide useful illustrations of some of the key issues that arise in relation to history on film. The first considered, *Lawrence of Arabia*, illustrates the degree to which a historical film may be based primarily on secondary, literary sources rather than on primary historical evidence, and how the differing priorities of history, literature and film can affect the way that history is presented in the film. The analysis of *Gangs of New York* in the second case study gives a slightly different slant to this meeting of different discourses – historical, literary and generic – in the historical film. In looking at this film we shall focus on the way that source materials – both secondary literary and primary historical ones – are re-worked through a specifically filmic frame of reference that draws heavily on a cinematic heritage that provides the visual language with which the film's narrative and historical elements are articulated. The final result is a film that, although apparently rich in historical detail, finally owes a great deal more to cinema than to history and consistently subordinates historical concerns to its cinematic imperatives.

The final section of the chapter takes a slightly different approach to some of the issues arising from film's implicit claim to be a way of gaining an understanding of historical events. Picking up the argument that begins in the analysis of *Gangs of New York*, that historical narratives created through the predominantly visual medium of film are shaped more by the codes and conventions of feature films and television drama than by strictly 'accurate' observance of historical 'facts', this section looks at some of the representational techniques employed in a group of films that share as a common theme the events of 9/11. Although conventional views of history require that there be a certain temporal remove between events and a historical recounting of them, this part of the chapter argues that, in a modern, mass-mediated culture, the impetus to historicise these events – to transform the chaotic and meaningless events themselves into a coherent narrative that claims to tell the 'truth' of the events and begins to place them in a wider context – is apparent even in the news footage that aired while the events themselves were still taking place. And since all histories are written from the perspective of the present, it would be a mistake to artificially separate these contemporary representations of these events from the histories yet to be written. Rather, what this case study illustrates is the need to see history as a continuous process of writing and re-writing the events of the past, a process that may begin almost at the very moment when an event of sufficient significance takes place.

'History isn't made up of truth anyhow, so why worry?'[1]

In the spring of 2004, *Cineaste* published a list of its editors' choices of their favourite historical films. Appearing in this chart at number 7 was David Lean's *Lawrence of Arabia*, a movie that most people would probably agree, with little hesitation, is a historical movie. However, in considering the validity of this historiographical claim – how closely the film actually reflects the life of T. E. Lawrence and the real historical events in which he was a participant – it is instructive to look at the nature of the sources of information about Lawrence's life and times that were used by the film-makers, and at the evolution of the project to depict Lawrence's life on the cinema screen.

Lean's film was made in 1962, but the idea of making a film about the life of Lawrence existed for a considerable time before that. Kevin Brownlow's biography of Lean reports a claim by film producer Herbert Wilcox that Lawrence visited him in 1926 to discuss the possibility of making a biographical film (1997: 405). What exactly transpired between Wilcox and Lawrence is ambiguous, however. Wilcox claims that he believed that Lawrence's life would not have made a good film, which, as Brownlow points out, seems highly unlikely. On the other hand, Lawrence's dislike for cinema is well documented and it is possible that he simply rebuffed Wilcox's advances. A letter Lawrence wrote to the film director Rex Ingram in 1927 clearly records his hope that there would never be a film of his life:

> Hollywood offered £6,000 or something, which the trustees turned down. Long may they go on turning it down. I'd hate to see myself parodied on the pitiful basis of my record of what the fellows with me did.[2]

Notwithstanding Lawrence's apparent antipathy towards the idea of a film about his life, numerous attempts were made by various industry figures between the late 1920s and the mid-1950s to overcome the numerous objections to such a project (see Brownlow 1997: 406–7). When the last of these other projects collapsed in 1955, producer Sam Spiegel set about acquiring the rights to Lawrence's own account of his involvement in the Arab revolt, published in his book *Seven Pillars of Wisdom*. Spiegel commissioned Michael Wilson, who had written the screenplay for Lean's earlier film, *Bridge on the River Kwai* (1957), to begin work on a screenplay for the film, with a view to persuading Professor A. W. Lawrence – T. E. Lawrence's brother and the trustee of his literary estate – to sell him the rights to *Seven Pillars*.[3] Since Spiegel did not own the rights to *Seven Pillars* at the time Wilson started writing the screenplay, his script was initially based on Lowell Thomas's account of Lawrence's involvement in the Arab revolt, *With Lawrence in Arabia,* and several of the biographies of Lawrence that had been published (Brownlow 1997: 408). The treatment Wilson produced impressed A. W. Lawrence, so much so that he agreed to sell the film rights to *Seven Pillars* to Spiegel. Following the acquisition of these rights, Wilson immediately started working on the new script, using *Seven Pillars* as its primary source. Later on, Robert Bolt replaced Wilson as screenwriter, but *Seven Pillars* remained the backbone of the screenplay.

There is scant evidence in the papers contained in the David Lean Collection held by the British Film Institute of any historical research that may have been undertaken by members of the film crew into aspects of the film that might be the subject of detailed research of this sort; particularly costumes and locations.[4] There is, however, ample evidence that the major source of inspiration, ideas and material for the film was literary from the outset. A document produced by Lean in October 1959 and titled 'Possible Scenes, Sequences, Characters or Visuals' (hereafter called *Possible Scenes*) gives a clear indication of the precise literary sources of key scenes in the film and of the way in which the main character and the narrative themes were developed. However, as *Possible Scenes* indicates, even when several different sources provided detailed information about a particular event, there was still considerable room available for the exercise of the director's imagination, and it was this that played the determining role in shaping the final form of a scene.

One scene in the second half of the film, in which Lawrence is severely beaten by Turkish soldiers, provides an excellent example. The scene is referred to on page 3 of *Possible Scenes*, in which Lean identifies references to the incident on which it is based on page 452 of *Seven Pillars*, on page 205 of Richard Aldington's biography of Lawrence and in a letter written by Lawrence to Charlotte Shaw, held in the British Museum. The scene, as it appears in the movie, is thus based on both primary documents (Lawrence's letter) and secondary, literary accounts. It is clear from *Possible Scenes*, however, that Lean found the various sources contradictory and that he harboured some doubts about what exactly had actually taken place:

> Although I find it difficult to form a whole out of this nucleus, I feel there is one; and it is connected with many other hints and odds and ends from the various books read. (*Possible Scenes*: 3)

Faced with such a confusing picture of the event in the available sources, the director explicitly acknowledges his own role as the active agent constructing a coherent version of the event from the available fragments; 'I will have to put down various odds and ends and hope that they will add up into something' (*Possible Scenes*: 4). Although by no means identical to the way the event is recounted in the book, the scene that appears in the film sufficiently resembles the account of the event in *Seven Pillars* as to be immediately recognisable. In the film Lawrence is detained on the street and (along with several other men) is brought before a Turkish officer who dismisses the other detainees and exhibits a clear sexual interest in Lawrence. After enduring a certain amount of the officer's attention, Lawrence brings his knee up sharply into the officer's groin. He is then punished by the officer who has several of his subordinates stretch Lawrence over a bench and flog him with a cane. The scene as filmed condenses a longer sequence of events described by Lawrence in *Seven Pillars*. In the book he is initially taken before a Turkish officer, who conscripts him into the Turkish army. Lawrence then spends the day in the company of several soldiers before being taken to the Governor after darkness has fallen, a journey that consists of a march through the town and across some railway tracks. According to Lawrence's account in *Seven Pillars* it is the Governor rather than the army officer who attempts to seduce the Englishman. The beating that concludes the account in the book is both more drawn-out and more brutal than that which appears in the movie. Although this scene clearly has its basis in fact, then, the film's presentation of the events in question does not follow exactly the sequence set out by Lawrence in

Seven Pillars, particularly in its compression of time and its condensation of two persons – the Turkish officer and the Governor – into one composite character.

This way of treating characters – taking two or more real people and transforming them into a more general type – is a distinct feature of *Lawrence of Arabia*. While many of the characters in the film represent real people, several others are purely fictional, composite figures, each modelled on several real people and functioning in the film as metaphors for abstract concepts relevant to the subject matter of the movie. Screenwriter Robert Bolt freely acknowledges that these characters were invented by him for this purpose in his introduction to the unpublished screenplay for *Lawrence of Arabia*. According to Bolt, Dryden 'represents European political skills' (Turner 1999: 508); Brighton's presence signals the ambivalence of Lawrence's character, the 'half admiring, half appalled disturbance raised by Lawrence in minds quite wedded to the admirable and inadequate code of English decency' (1999: 509). Auda 'is meant to be Brighton's Bedouin equivalent' (ibid.). Ali signifies 'emergent Arab nationalism' (1999: 508), while Bentley represents the press, and 'worldly experience and cynical wisdom' that contrasts with and thus gives emphasis to the idealism that Lawrence himself represents (see Wilson 2006). While there can be little doubt that the abstract themes conveyed through these characters are relevant to the narrative development of the film, the construction of these characters is an explicitly figurative device that removes the film a further degree from the historical events it depicts than even the literary sources on which the film is based. It is clear from this analysis of the sources that informed the development of *Lawrence of Arabia* that any connection the film has to the historical events to which it ostensibly refers was mediated from the outset by the literary codes and conventions that shaped the source materials upon which the film was directly based. And while film scholars may still be eager to praise the film as an exemplar of historical filmmaking, its makers were under no illusions about the film's priorities when it came to striking a balance between historical and dramatic concerns. Lean's production notes are quite explicit about the fact that the prime motivation of the film was dramatic rather than historical. And while the plot of the film would endeavour to follow the historical 'facts' where possible, the director would not hesitate to substitute a fictional narrative for a historically accurate one whenever the overarching dramatic concerns of the film demanded it:

On first reading of Villars version of the fighting before Damascus
I gained an erroneous impression which I passed on to Sam and
Mike on the boat, and I want to correct it in case it sticks. I said
that in this final slaughter of the Turks Lawrence became a horri-
fied spectator of 'savages whose instincts had been set free'. On
second reading I think it is quite wrong. At first I was sorry to dis-
cover this, thinking the fiction better than the truth. Now I think the
truth is better, unless of course, the character-line of the film calls
for fiction. (*Possible Scenes*: 11)

Bolt too felt little need to attempt to deny the film's limitations as a representation of the historical events it depicts. As he freely acknowledged,
the primary source for his screenplay was *Seven Pillars*; itself a highly
subjective, narrative construction of the events it recounts, and one that
Bolt suggests is regarded by 'some authorities' as in parts 'untrue or so
highly coloured as to be virtually untrue' (Turner 1999: 505). Even Lawrence
himself acknowledged the highly subjective position from which *Seven
Pillars* was written: 'the history is not of the Arab movement, but of me in
it' (1962: 22).

Another factor that limits *Lawrence of Arabia*'s claim to be a presentation of history arises from the need to select which of the numerous events
and characters in *Seven Pillars* to include in the screen version. *Seven
Pillars* presents an extremely 'diffuse and detailed' account of a particular
period in Lawrence's life (Bolt in Turner 1999: 505), and its narrative greatly
exceeds what it would be possible to present in a commercial feature film,
even one as long as *Lawrence of Arabia*. The process of selecting which
events in the book would be reproduced on the screen is one which Bolt
acknowledged was an 'impudent exercise', but one which nevertheless
'must be done' (ibid.). Thus the screenwriter was required to make subjective decisions about the relative importance of the various events described
in the book when composing the screenplay. This choice of which events
to include and which to omit is one which removes the film's screenplay
a further degree from the original source material. These choices, as Bolt
acknowledged 'will depend on yourself, not Lawrence, who at this point
is made helpless' (in Turner 1999: 505–6). This need to adopt a selective
approach to the source material in the process of adaptation magnifies the
already-existing disparity between the version of events presented in the

film and the historical realities, as a remark in a letter from Lean to Spiegel, acknowledging the differences between his vision of events and the facts of the historical campaign, illustrates:

> I see one, or perhaps two, train wrecks and am therefore astounded when I am told that in the real campaign there were something like eighty.[5]

And it is quite clear from this letter that, like Bolt, Lean recognised the nature of his role as being that of a story teller rather than that of historian. Lean continues:

> It is rather as if we had taken the Old Testament, fastened on a string of incidents which took our fancy, and put it out as a film version of the whole. Of course this is not a very good example, but it's just about what we've done with *Seven Pillars*. We can't show all the scenes in 3 hours, but I think we ought to tell the audience we are not attempting to do so, for if we don't they'll miss the sweep of the campaign as it actually was.[6]

Although a historical film like *Lawrence of Arabia* may be based on real people and events, both the film's screenwriter and it's director were quite clear that what they were presenting on screen did not amount to a history – in the traditional sense – of the period and events depicted. Like more conventional forms of history, however, the film was motivated by the concerns of the period in which it was produced more than those in which it is set. Bolt acknowledges as much in his apologia:

> Historical plays (and screenplays) afford historical evidence not of the lives and times they purport to display but rather of the lives and times which produced them. Richard III tells us little that is reliable about Gloucester and the 15th century but a lot about Shakespeare and Elizabethan England. (Turner 1999: 506)

While it is true that it is possible that there may be additional documents yet to be discovered relating to the production of *Lawrence of Arabia* that could further illuminate the filmmakers' concerns with historical matters, it is clear from the currently available documents the filmmakers were less concerned with faithful adherence to the historical details of the events presented in the film than with the need to produce a compelling and dramatic film based, in very general terms, on Lawrence's involvement in the Arab revolt. While the film may have a historical kernel, it is fleshed out by a great deal of purely fictional material that represents a substantial departure from the historical realities of Lawrence's life. Its basis is primarily literary, then, rather than historical and while this may allow the filmmakers to produce a type of historical narrative that is consistent with the vision of historical writing suggested by Slotkin, for example, it is very clear from this brief examination of the source materials, and the uses made of them by the filmmakers, that the effectiveness of this type of historical narrative on film is achieved only at the cost of significant departures from the historical realities of the events and persons depicted in the movie.

History, drama and the 'language' of cinema: Gangs of New York

Despite the fact that many aspects of *The Birth of a Nation* are politically regressive and unpalatable for the majority of film viewers today, there is no doubt that, from the perspective of the filmmakers, the movie represented a genuine attempt to present on film a historical account of aspects of the development of a distinct sense of American nationhood in the period following the Civil War. That our understanding of the history of the period in question has altered since the time of the film's production, and our attitudes towards race have changed dramatically in no way alters the fact that Griffith and his collaborators believed that they were presenting a true account of the periods in question. Although having a concern with different geographical settings, and different characters and events than Griffith's film, Martin Scorsese's *Gangs of New York* represents a recent cinematic rendition of this period of American history and, like *The Birth of a Nation*, *Gangs of New York* is centrally concerned with the development of nationhood in America. As I will demonstrate in this part of the chapter, although Scorsese's movie may not be as obviously repugnant to modern political and cultural sensibilities, *Gangs of New York* hardly shows greater concern with empirical historical detail than did D. W. Griffith's film in 1915.

The opening scenes of *Gangs of New York* are set in 1846 and are mainly concerned with establishing the physical setting in which the drama of the main part of the film – which begins some 16 years later, in 1862, the second year of the Civil War – will take place. The setting is Five Points, an impoverished slum neighbourhood in lower Manhattan[7] that is home to various groups of recent immigrants to the USA,[8] as well as American 'natives'.[9] The locale enjoyed considerable notoriety during the nineteenth century for its associations with crime, violence, prostitution and drunkenness. Conflict between the various 'gangs' that occupied the neighbourhood was common, and an instance of the clashes that occurred is presented on a spectacular scale in the film's opening scenes, which graphically depict nothing less than a full-scale battle between a gang of Protestant 'natives' and an alliance of Irish Catholic gangs, both factions vying for control of the Five Points.

The film's ending is set immediately after the draft riots of 1863. However, this and the other historical events and characters based on real people who lived in the neighbourhood at various times merely provide a background. Against this background the film's two narrative strands – Amsterdam Vallon's (Leonardo Di Caprio) quest for revenge against William 'Bill the Butcher' Cutting (Daniel Day Lewis) for the killing of Amsterdam's father, and the romance that develops between Amsterdam and Jenny Everdeane (Cameron Diaz) – are played out.[10] The shift in emphasis between a film that is 'about' historical events and one that merely uses these to establish the *mise-en-scène* within which an explicitly fictional narrative takes place may be a fairly subtle one for many moviegoers. It is, however, a crucial one when considering whether the film can be regarded as a reliable depiction of the historical period. The film's director, Martin Scorsese, has been quite explicit that his intention was not to produce a historiographical movie; 'This is based on history. There's no doubt about it. But it is still a film that is more of an opera than history'.[11] As the director explains the process of producing the screenplay:

> we composed a personal story that revolved around the classic theme of revenge. We based some of our characters on real-life people and created others. We also took dramatic license by moving a few dates and places. (Anon. 2003: 20)

Jay Cocks, one of the film's screenwriters, has been equally forthright about the uses made of history in the movie. The film is ostensibly based on Herbert Asbury's 1927 non-fiction book, *The Gangs of New York*, but according to Cocks the film 'doesn't follow the Asbury book at all. We supplied the story. Asbury supplied inspiration and a little history.' Indeed the book appears to have supplied little more than inspiration for the imaginations of the film's creators; Cocks admits that the book

> gave us the chance to be Ned Buntline [creator of the dime novel]. Make up our own myths, based in history ... But lies and falsehoods can often be more helpful to drama than fact. (Quoted in Anon. 2002)

While the director's and screenwriter's explicit denials of any historiographical intent provide convenient defences against claims of distortion and historical inaccuracy, and while their disavowal may provide some excuse for inattention to the minutiae of historical events, it is difficult for the makers of a film that is in some way based on historical facts to escape the demands of historical fidelity so easily. Numerous demands for accurate attention to historical detail arise from the *mise-en-scène* itself, particularly in relation to the elaboration of the physical environment in which the action takes place, as well as the costumes, argot and demeanour of the characters. So far as these aspects of the film are concerned, notwithstanding the denials of responsibility for historical accuracy, there is ample evidence that considerable historical research was undertaken. Although production of the film began in 2001, Scorsese and Cocks had been working on it for a considerable time before production commenced; since the early 1970s. In the intervening years the director amassed a substantial collection of research materials relating to the historical aspects of the film. In addition to the director's own research, a historical consultant – Luc Sante, author of *Low Life: The Lures and Snares of Old New York* – was brought in to advise the production team. Furthermore, occasional advice on factual matters was also sought from Tyler Anbinder, professor of history at George Washington University and the author of *Five Points* (2002), a cultural history of the neighbourhood; and from an archaeologist, Rebecca Yamin, who had led the team that had analysed and documented 850,000 artefacts unearthed during construction work in the old Five Points neighbourhood between 1992 and 1998.[12] Despite the concern with accurate historical detail that would appear to be implicit in the engagement of this

Paradise Square set: *Gangs of New York*

array of learned historical consultants, the film's rendering of history has been criticised by many historians, including both Anbinder and Yamin. Sante is the only historical consultant involved in the making of the film who has not voiced some concern about its depiction of life in Five Points at the time in question.

Both Anbinder and Yamin have acknowledged that certain aspects of *Gangs of New York* represent a very powerful evocation of the atmosphere of the Five Points neighbourhood during the mid-nineteenth century. For example Anbinder, Yamin and others have praised the main set, Paradise Square, the centre of the Five Points intersection, which was reconstructed full scale at the Cinecittà Studio outside Rome. In an interview, Anbinder and Yamin both acknowledge the achievement of the set designer in faithfully reproducing the appearance of the physical environment of Paradise Square in the mid-nineteenth century.[13] This is a judgement with which historian Vincent DiGirolamo concurs: 'The real stars of the movie are the spectacular sets' (2004: 126). Anbinder particularly praises the design of the set for its evocation of the place and time, the 'buildings looked almost exactly like they would have looked. You get a good sense of the griminess, the dirtiness of the street.' However, Yamin's comment that 'the physical set ... is right out of Dickens' underscores the limitations of the film's superficial verisimilitude.[14] Dickens and other social commentators visited Five Points in the mid-nineteenth century and wrote about the depraved conditions they found there. These accounts may have helped the filmmakers to achieve striking verisimilitude in constructing the exterior sets but, as

Old Brewery interior: *Gangs of New York*

Yamin remarks, while the filmmakers could build a convincing reproduction of the street-facing aspect of the neighbourhood, they 'couldn't see inside the lives of the people who lived inside those decrepit houses' because 'those apartments ... were only seen from the outside by those middle-class people who wrote those descriptions' (quoted in Chamberlain 2003). In another interview, Anbinder also highlights the limitations of the set. When asked for his views about the interior of the Old Brewery building, Anbinder remarks:

> No one knows what it looked like inside. It did not have the big, open spaces shown in the movie. No landlord would let all that space go to waste. Descriptions from the time say it was carved up into little cubicles to fit as many tenants in the tenement as possible. (*Gotham Gazette* 2002)

The same point could be made about any of the film's interior sets. In the same interview Jay Cocks remarks that the set for the interior of the Old Brewery was a product of the imagination of the filmmakers rather than an attempt to recreate the real location. However, it is clear that this set, like many aspects of the movie, owed much to the sets used in other films, which also formed an important element in the research material used by the makers of *Gangs of New York*. The filmmakers' imagination was thus fuelled by a distinctively cinematic representational heritage that inter-sects with the film's historical dimension to produce its vision of period and geographical setting. Of the many films viewed by the filmmakers in preparation for the production of *Gangs of New York*, the influence of one of these, *Oliver Twist* (1948) – which features several sets with the type of large, open interiors and wooden staircases that define the interior of the Old Brewery – is evident. The influence of other movies on the design of the interior sets in *Gangs of New York* is also apparent in the case of Sparrow's Chinese Pagoda which, as Scorsese acknowledges (Anon. 2002: 44), was influenced by night-club interiors in Josef von Sternberg's *The Shanghai Gesture* (1941).[15]

While it is true, as Yamin notes, that contemporaneous accounts of the smaller details of the lives of the people who inhabited the tenements of the Five Points are not available, either to academic historians or to the filmmakers, certain details of how those lives were lived can be gleaned from the archaeological record of the area. However, even where these details were ascertainable, the filmmakers often ignored the realities. By way of an example, Yamin argues that while the film emphasises the utter squalor of the lives of Five Points inhabitants, the impression gained from

Nightclub interior: *The Shanghai Gesture*

Sparrow's Chinese Pagoda interior: *Gangs of New York*

the archaeological and historical records suggest that the reality was far less sordid, with many residents aspiring to a more middle-class type of respectability; 'They had ornaments on their mantels and pictures on their walls and teapots and teacups, and they were eating very well' (Yamin quoted in Chamberlain 2003). According to Yamin, the Five Points bore no resemblance to the film's more extreme visions of everyday life in the neighbourhood:

> In the Scorsese movie you have these scenes in a basement where there are skulls in the corners and people are draped in rags … We didn't see anything to suggest that people were living like that. There were certainly no skulls rolling around in people's rooms. (Ibid.)

The inclusion of these details in the film indicates the importance of the filmmakers' imaginations in constructing the fictional diegetic world portrayed in the movie. At the same time the filmmakers neglected factual details upon which advice had been given by the scholars they consulted. This combination of the inclusion of imaginary details and the omission of factual ones clearly signals the filmmakers' priorities. If there is some sense of tension in the film between visual impact and drama on the one hand, and historical accuracy on the other, it is clear that precedence is given to the former. Yamin provides an example of this. She and her team advised movie researchers about period furnishings and had shown them small glass tumblers that were typically used for drinking in the Five Points in the period in question. When Yamin saw the film, however

> the thing I really noticed was those pewter mugs everyone was drinking out of. Well, they stopped drinking out of those in the 18th century ... In other words, they didn't learn anything from us. (Ibid.)

A similar observation could be made of another aspect of *Gangs of New York* that was extensively researched by members of the film's production team but which, in the realisation, deviated significantly from the course of historical accuracy: the costumes. Costume designer, Sandy Powell, undertook extensive research into the dress of the period, using contemporary paintings and daguerreotypes as reference sources, but admits that

> a lot of what we've done isn't strictly historically correct. We went through various stages and it does end up getting fairly stylised as well. All being based with historical accuracy, I've then taken it a few steps further. (*Gangs of New York* DVD special features)

The overall effect of the costumes is one of general historical verisimilitude. They are not obviously anachronistic, but neither do they accurately reproduce in detail the sort of clothing that Five Points residents would have worn in the mid-nineteenth century. This contradictory mix of historical accuracy and clear inattention to the minutiae of historical detail is consistent with Anbinder's final verdict on the film's rendering of history; 'the overall theme is what he most got right',[16] but 'in terms of the specifics, you don't want to rely on the movie'.[17]

Despite the filmmakers' evident concern with the process of undertaking historical research for the movie, *Gangs of New York* finally exhibits similar characteristics to many other attempts to render history on film. These include compression of complicated details into simplified but visually impressive tableaux, temporal and geographical relocation of actual events in order to assimilate them into the dramatic narrative of the movie, and simplification of complicated historical characters into more generalised 'types' that fit better within the intersecting and often contradictory imperatives – including the available historical data but also specifically filmic factors such as genre and the director's oeuvre – that determine a film's representational modes. However, the invocation of the idea of history in a film amounts to an assertion of special status as against other, purely fictional, feature films that claim to be nothing more than entertainment. The historical feature film occupies a middle-ground somewhere between these entertainment features and the scholarly written histories from which historical films selectively pick choice details in order to insert them into representational modes of the former; a simultaneous decontextualisation of events (from history) and recontextualisation (within the filmic regimes of narrative, genre and so on) that enables movies to preserve the appearance of historicity while discarding all of the rigour demanded of the academic historian. As DiGirolamo observes:

> authenticity to a filmmaker is largely getting the look of a movie to correspond to what most people think is the look of the period. It means lifting details from other movies *about* the period as well as from source material *of* the period; hence the susceptibility to anachronism and stereotype. (2004: 134)

But popular feature films and arcane academic histories do not rank equally in the production of our consciousness of the past. The evocative power of the lavish, expensively produced visual imagery available to the historical filmmaker inevitably outweighs the less immediately impressive medium employed by the historical scholar. Additionally, as DiGirolamo observes, historical feature films tend to confirm existing popular conceptions of the past while academic historians tend to challenge these. These factors together create a strong predisposition for the version of historical events presented in the movies to become the accepted, popular 'truth' about the past. In one of his interviews about his involvement in the making of *Gangs of New York*, Anbinder expresses his concerns about precisely this tendency in the film:

> what one fears is that these images, because they are visual and so memorable and stick in people's minds, it will be impossible

'no rivers of blood running through the city': the 1863 draft riots as seen in *Gangs of New York*

for them to remember that there were no ships firing in the harbor during the draft riots and no rivers of blood running through the city. Those are the kinds of things that are going to be hard for people to delete from their memory. (Quoted in Bartolomeo 2003)

Others have been even more robust in their criticisms of the movie. In an online review of Astbury's and Anbinder's books, for example, Paul Gilje condemns the film for what he sees as an distortion of historical facts; 'millions have had their image of the Five Points warped by the cinematography of Martin Scorsese' (2003).

The tendency of historical feature films to present a simplified and hyperbolic version of the past is undoubtedly a legitimate cause for concern for anyone interested in the enterprise of historical study. Before condemning the historical feature film as an almost unadulterated fantasy that compares unfavourably with other modes of ostensibly factual narrative, however, it is worth considering the degree to which the same tendencies and representational modes encountered in the historical feature film are pervasive throughout the mass mediated culture in which we now live. In particular it is instructive to consider how these modes shape the presentation of real events of historical significance within other genres of visual media that are far less often challenged in their role as chroniclers of historical fact.

"...it looked like a movie": 9/11, 'live' news and film history

At 8.46 A.M. on 11 September 2001 a hijacked aeroplane, American Airlines Flight 11 from Boston to Los Angeles, collided with the North Tower of the World Trade Center in New York. Within minutes the eyes of the world were turned towards this building in lower Manhattan through the lenses of multiple television news agencies that began broadcasting live coverage of the event from a number of vantage points around New York City and the surrounding areas. The news broadcasters' response to events was extremely rapid and within minutes they had set up numerous live feeds of images filmed from different positions around New York and New Jersey, which were providing footage to support the commentary of the news anchors. As a result of the speed of their response, by the time United Airlines Flight 175 struck the South Tower, seconds before 9.03 A.M., a large number of news cameras – as well of those of numerous amateurs who had turned their video cameras towards the shocking spectacle – were filming the smoking North Tower and inadvertently captured the last moments of the second plane's approach to and collision with the South Tower. Throughout that day, and those that followed, the attention of the world's news media remained focused on the developing events in lower Manhattan. A common observation made by several of the 'eye-witnesses' to the events was that 'it seemed like it wasn't even real' as one by-stander interviewed by CNN commented or, as New York Fire Department Battalion Chief, Steve Grabher put it, the scene 'looked like a movie'.

Although this may seem to be a strange reaction to events that must have been all too real to those on the scene, it is less surprising when we consider the relative frequency with which images of spectacular destruction on the kind of scale which occurred that morning are encountered in Hollywood movies. Faced with a catastrophic and barely comprehensible event, it is hardly surprising that onlookers reframed the event in terms of the only context in which they had encountered anything of the sort before and utilised the familiar representational context of the movies as a lens through which events could be rendered comprehensible and discussed. As Geoff King has observed, 'a very real event was experienced – at least in part – through a frame provided by Hollywood spectacle' (2005: 47).

If the events of that morning appeared to those at the scene to be more easily comprehensible when conceptualised in terms of Hollywood's

familiar repertoire of representational techniques, the sense of experiencing the events as if they were a movie was probably even more pronounced for those watching the events unfold on 'live' television news
throughout the day. Adding to the already cinematic magnitude of the
disaster, as the news broke and as more footage of the collisions became
available during the course of the morning's uninterrupted news broadcasts, broadcasters began to edit together the separate fragments of film
footage being fed from all over the city, applying continuity editing principles to them in order to construct a coherent narrative – a 'cinematic
assemblage of images' (King 2005: 51) – from these smaller units. The
news broadcasters made use of a 'match-on-action, a standard device
from the conventions of cinematic and televisual continuity editing, to
establish a seamless cut from one image to the other' (ibid.). An example
of this technique can be observed in one of the reports broadcast by CNN
later in the day. The part of the report dealing with the crashing of the
second plane into the South Tower begins with a long shot filmed from
a vantage point further uptown, approximately north-east of the World
Trade Center, showing the two towers just before the second collision,
the North Tower ablaze as United Airlines flight 175 (barely more than
a moving dot on the screen at this distance) enters the shot from the
right hand side. As the plane moves towards the building there is a cut
to a closer shot, this time filmed from a different uptown position, closer
to due north from the World Trade Center, from which vantage point the
South Tower is completely obscured from view by the North Tower. This
shot continues until the plane collides with the building and explodes,
at which point there is a cut to yet another shot, filmed from a position
to the east of the site, possibly in Brooklyn, showing both towers at the
moment of the explosion caused by the collision between Flight 175 and
the South Tower. In this news report these three pieces of footage, filmed
independently of each other and from different geographical perspectives, are joined according to classical Hollywood principles of continuity
editing to make out of these fragmentary pieces of filmed historical data a
more meaningful and coherent narrative whole. Although the news coverage of these events should not be regarded as an attempt to 'write' a history of 9/11, analysis of the formal principles applied to the organisation
of the news coverage is instructive. It reveals the process of mediation
through which the visible traces of historical events are transformed into

CNN footage shows U.A.175 approaching the World Trade Center...

...then cuts to a different shot for a closer view as the plane closes on the building...

...and finally cuts to a third shot to show the explosion resulting from the impact

a narrative about those events through their juxtaposition with each other within a genre of discourse (in this case 'news') which claims to present the 'truth' about the event.

In the case of this news coverage, the combination of the immediacy of the individual pieces of footage with the narrative dimension provided by the use of continuity editing produces a short sequence of film that has a powerful visual impact and a strong sense of realism. Few watching the news coverage of the events as they occurred would have questioned its truthfulness. The process of mediation here identified as being at work in the production of this short sequence of film – the collapsing of different perspectives together to produce a single, coherent narrative – is, however, an example of the process of translating raw events into a discourse, a process that, on a larger scale, closely approximates the historiographical activity of contextualising key events within a wider array of social, political and economic forces. Although too little time has passed since the events of 9/11 for a suitably distanced historical perspective to have developed, there have already been numerous books and official documents published that claim to reveal the truth about those events. Taking into consideration the way that contemporaneous television news coverage of 9/11 was evidently shaped by formal principles derived from narrative cinema, it is possible to see that the process of translation of events into a discourse or discourses began almost immediately after the first plane struck the North tower. It has since operated in different genres of discourse – breaking news, news-analysis, official reports, non-fiction literature and so on – at varying degrees of remove from the events themselves, with the live television news coverage being the most proximate and the rigorous, objective scholarly history, which is yet to be written, among the furthest removed. Between these extremes lie the numerous other attempts to relate the story of 9/11, including 'official' version of the events contained in *The 9/11 Commission Report* (2004) and the various films that have been produced, including the made-for-television movies and docudramas, *Let's Roll: The Story of Flight 93* (2002), *World Trade Center: Anatomy of the Collapse* (2002), *The Flight That Fought Back* (2005) and *Flight 93* (2006), as well as the feature films intended for cinema release, such as *United 93* (2006) and *World Trade Center* (2006). What is instructive about these filmed accounts of the events that occupy a middle ground between the immediacy of the news coverage and the distance

Television news as authenticating presence: *Flight 93* and *United 93*

expected of history, is the way that they all employ basically the same representational techniques that were observed in the news coverage in order
to construct a narrative that is simultaneously both based on real historical
events and yet also a fictionalisation. *Flight 93*, *United 93* and *The Flight
That Fought Back* all incorporate some of the actual news coverage of
the event, with the use of television sets within the diegesis, as a way of
asserting the authenticity of their (fictionalised) accounts of the events.
The latter film goes the furthest in staking its claim to authenticity, using
actual audio material taken from the recordings made of transmissions
from the hijacked plane and from telephone calls made by passengers to

their families in order to anchor its fictional dramatisation of events within the plane to the historical reality of the events themselves. At the same time, *The Flight That Fought Back* also features the most explicit use, in any of these films, of highly stylised representational techniques derived from contemporary television drama. Narrated by the actor Kiefer Sutherland and occasionally employing a digital clock onscreen and a split screen technique that allows multiple perspectives to be presented simultaneously, the visual style of *The Flight That Fought Back* references the popular television action drama, *24* (2001–present), to provide viewers with interpretive cues as to the filmmakers' preferred reading of the film.

These films based on the events of 9/11, illustrate how difficult it is finally to judge a movie as historiography. The films have a basis in historical fact and foreground that basis as a way of staking their claims to authenticity and truthfulness. Yet they also involve a significant degree of fictionalisation and are created within generic and institutional structures that impose demands other than pure historical veracity upon them, and which can lead to distortion and historical inaccuracy. The effect of these competing forces on the films certainly means that they cannot be regarded as substitutes for rigorous, scholarly written histories, and they will always compare unfavourably with these academic works when judged by the standards usually applied to the academic history. Nevertheless, it is likely that films such as these will prove to be the dominant source of information regarding the events of 9/11 for the majority of the population and therein lies the potential danger of history on film; the danger that public knowledge of historical events will be formed by accounts that are created under the pressure of forces that are not governed by historiographical intent and the rigorous standards expected of academic histories.

Conclusions

The three case studies contained in this chapter all examine feature films that have been shaped in one way or another by real historical events and/ or persons. The films discussed may be very different in their subject matter and style, but in all of the case studies a similar pattern emerges insofar as the process of translating real events into their onscreen rendition is concerned. *Lawrence of Arabia* is based on events that really occurred and its characters – at least some of them – are modelled on people who really lived and participated in those events. However, the main sources of information the filmmakers have used in creating the film are not original, material traces of the past depicted in the film, nor even scholarly histories that have those material traces as their basis, but biographical and autobiographical accounts, which are frequently more interested in legend-building than with faithfully representing the events and persons concerned. The 'history' presented in *Lawrence of Arabia* is thus twice mediated − firstly by the source materials and secondly by the film itself − and so doubly distanced from the events which it portrays. Additionally, since each round of mediation involves an encounter between the facts of history and the generic rules that govern the form within which those facts will be presented as a historical narrative, it is not difficult to see that history on film presents a problem for film scholars and historians alike.

The effects of this problem are especially acute in the case of *Gangs of New York*, in which the triumph of generic and media-specific modes of presentation over the (admittedly extensively researched) facts of history that the film takes as its basis is particularly clear. *Gangs of New York* may take from history the facts that the Five Points neighbourhood was a slum, that it had a large immigrant population and that it was the scene of fights between rival gangs, but these historical fragments are rendered onscreen using an intertextual visual mode that is specifically filmic. *Oliver Twist* provides a way of visually coding the slum neighbourhood; *The Shanghai Gesture* provides a code for the Chinese immigrants who, in reality arrived in the numbers shown in the film after the period in which the movie is set; and a range of other films, including *The Wild Bunch* (1969) and *A Clockwork Orange* (1971) provide a way of visually coding the gangs and their behaviour. Thus filtered through the lens of film history, the history of life in the Five Points diminishes in relative magnitude, to the point where the few details of history that remain can only be seen as a mere inspiration for the film rather than its basis.

It may seem a fairly trivial matter to worry about how reliably history is presented in what is, after all, quite clearly a form of entertainment. But the problems cannot be dismissed so lightly when the popular reach and evocative power of the film and television so greatly exceeds that of the 'serious' academic history. Nor is there much comfort to be gained from the postmodernists' recognition that even the scholarly historical work is an act of writing involving creative and selective processes. This may be true but, as the first two case studies in this chapter demonstrate, the factual basis of an ostensibly historical film may prove to be rather thin and somewhat distanced from the original sources of historical data that the rigorous academic history takes as its basis.

The subject matter of the final case study in this chapter provides an excellent example in support of the argument that it is important that the public consciousness of the truth of a historical event should be shaped by historical narratives (whether filmed or written) that are concerned to ascertain (as far as possible) what did happen and to faithfully render a reliable version of history. Although the early news coverage of the events of 9/11 had only piecemeal fragments of footage upon which to base its reports, the organisation of those fragments into a more coherent visual narrative, constructed according to the classical Hollywood principles of continuity editing, was evident even on the day of the events themselves. The television news media started to shift from a purely reactive mode early in the day, when they could only show what was going on, to a narrative mode in which they began the attempt to tell the story of the events.

One of the things that analysis of the news coverage on 9/11 and of some of the subsequent films based on the events of that day reveals is that the making of a history is a process that is ongoing and continuous. While the initial draft of this chapter was being written, *United 93* was still playing in cinemas and *World Trade Center* was about to be released in the UK. It would have been possible to delay writing this draft for a few weeks in order to include a discussion of Stone's movie. However, there would have been little gained by this delay since the inclusion of *World Trade Center* would not bring our understanding of the events of 9/11 any closer to a state of historical completion. There is always another film to be made, another book to be written that moves the end of history further out of reach. Including Stone's movie would only emphasise the absence of the next, as yet unmade, effort to render the events of 9/11 on screen.

That it is positively desirable to refrain from imposing an ending upon a history that is necessarily evolving is well illustrated by the final shot in Steven Spielberg's *Munich*. The film is a fictionalised account of the activities of a covert Israeli assassination squad given the task of hunting down a number of Palestinians believed to be responsible for the kidnapping and killing of the Israeli Olympic team in 1972. At the film's conclusion a meeting takes place near the waterfront in Queens, New York between

A teleological vision of events leading to 9/11: *Munich*

Amer (Eric Bana), the leader of the hit squad and Ephraim (Geoffrey Rush), the man who assigned them the task. As the men part company and Amer walks away, the camera follows him briefly before stopping to dwell on the sight of the twin towers of the World Trade Center, now digitally reinserted into the Manhattan skyline; the film's final image. In this simple shot that occupies the screen for a few seconds only, *Munich* evokes a teleological vision of history, which implies a direct chain of causation that links the events of Munich in 1972 with those of 9/11. And while the history of troubled relations between Israel and Palestine has undoubtedly played a part in the development of conditions in which the events of 9/11 could take place, the direct causal relationship implied by this shot is simplistic and reductive. By implying an ending (the events of 9/11) to the narrative that unfolds in the film, *Munich* attempts to foreclose the process of meaning-making in a particular way, leading the audience towards the conclusion that the history of events leading up to 9/11 is a relatively simple and linear sequence beginning with the kidnapping of the Olympic team in 1972 and continuing through the events shown in the film and then onwards through a series of events that take place after the film's concluding point, events that are not shown but are powerfully implied by that final image of the World Trade Center. This is the essence of the problem with the depiction of history on film, as it is actually realised in practice as opposed to its theoretical potential as a mode for rendering history. Based loosely on history but forgoing the complexities and contradictions of history in favour of other narrative and dramatic considerations, while also having an almost unique power to shape popular perceptions of what 'really happened', the historical film provides a seductive appearance of historicity that all too easily translates, in the popular imaginary, to a faithful rendition of historical events that, in reality, it can never be. For this reason attempts to represent history on film must always be regarded with a highly critical eye.

5   CONCLUSION

In this book I have not attempted to provide a comprehensive account of all the issues that arise when it comes to considering the complicated relationships between film and history. The focus of this book has been directed towards two particular areas within the broader field of film history: the use of films as documents of their historical period and their use as a way of writing the history of events in the past. The rationale for choosing to look at these, while ignoring other aspects of history and film, is that the two facets of history and film dealt with in this book are those which are most clearly implicated in the production and circulation of meanings. Histories of the changing technologies of film production and consumption, of particular studios, of specific directors and of the production of particular movies; all of these are fascinating matters for study and valuable contributions to our knowledge of the movies, but none is implicated in meaning-making, in the production of socially pervasive understandings of the past nearly as much as are the aspects of history discussed at length in this book. If film has such an influence on the moulding of our consciousness of the past then it is crucial that we adopt a critical and analytical stance towards it, that we interrogate its epistemological status, its reliability and its aptness to the task of informing our understanding of history. The aim of this book has been to introduce some of the important debates that attend this area of study and some of the tools that can be used in order to critically evaluate the version of history we obtain from films.

Chapters 1 and 2 have offered firstly a theoretical and then a more practical introduction to the use of films and other contemporary artefacts of the culture to try to understand what those films meant within the wider context of social, political, economic debates of their time; of medical, sexual, occupational and other discourses that can be traced through films and which allow later film researchers and cultural historians a glimpse of the issues that concerned and interested the people who formed the movie audiences of the time. This approach to historical film analysis is well illustrated by the case study of *Rear Window* in chapter 2. *Rear Window* is a film that scholars of film have previously understood primarily from either auteurist or psychoanalytic viewpoints, and I do not suggest that the analysis I offer in this book supersedes or negates either of these approaches. However, I do suggest that our understanding of what the film means is given a much sharper focus by the kind of historical analysis I undertake here. Viewed from the vantage point offered by materialist historical reception studies it would be possible – as well as understanding the film's meaning-making potential in its original context – to trace the diachronically changing meanings of the film as it is removed from one discursive context and repositioned within another at different times. Thus popularised medical discourses provide a discursive frame for the film in its original context in the mid-1950s; the auteurist discourses of early film studies provide a frame for the 1960s and the cine-psychoanalytic discourses that dominated film studies in the 1970s and early 1980s offer yet another historically specific instance of reception. None of these earlier ways that film studies has understood the film is wrong, therefore, but merely the result of the action upon the film text of a historically specific conjuncture of discourses. This is not to claim for historical reception studies the status of a kind of transcendental metacriticism; a 'final word' that definitively settles the meaning of the film once and for all. Rather it demonstrates that there is to be no 'end of history' here, that it is impossible to reach a final meaning that exhausts all possibilities for re-inserting the film into different discursive contexts that produce new, historically conditioned meanings for the film.

Chapters 3 and 4 examine the potential and the realities of the endeavour to employ film as a way of writing histories of past events. Since history does not have an existence independent of its writing and since film offers much greater potential for photo-realist representation of events – a chance to *see* what it was like rather than merely read about it – it seems that it ought to be the case that film offers the possibility for a far richer, more nuanced and immediate experience of history than the conventional written work. However, as the case studies in chapter 4 illustrate, this ideal of history on film is rarely realised in practice. Faced with pressures to render a compelling dramatic narrative, filmmakers routinely compress events into a shorter time span than that on which they really occurred, condense numerous real persons into invented composite characters designed to function as metaphors for larger themes relevant to the times and/or events depicted, and exaggerate aspects of costumes and sets in order to achieve a greater dramatic impact on the cinema screen. Whatever the potential of the medium, it seems that the reality of history on film fails to clear any but the lowest empirical hurdles on the road to acceptance as an alternative to the scholarly written history.

The final case study illustrates why any of this matters; why anyone should care how reliably history is represented on film. Taking a very recent event of enormous social and political magnitude as their subject, the films discussed in this case study continue the work begun in some of the news broadcasts of the day in question, spinning from fragments of information a compelling and convincing narrative that, for many viewers of these films, will become the 'truth' about these events, will become the history of 9/11; a history that may be relatively thin evidentially and over-reliant on too narrow a range of sources, and ones that are politically far from neutral and objective.[1]

Hamid Dabashi argues that the 'traumatic terror at the heart of the codification of "9/11"' should be read 'as a form of historical amnesia, a collective repression, that corresponds best with the globalised spectacle of its having made the apparently invulnerable evidently vulnerable' (2006). The events of 9/11 were just too traumatic, Dabashi suggests, to allow them to be remembered as they were, and the resulting collective repression of them has left a void too easily filled with fabulous tales of the events – filled with 'instantaneous enemies and moving targets' (ibid.) – that becomes the official version of the events and that might become its 'history' unless resisted. The inability of film to sustain a debate about history is one of the key reasons behind Ian Jarvie's dismissal of the medium as a way of 'doing' history and although there are efforts by some independent filmmakers to counter the effect of the official history-making evident in the movies about 9/11, the frequently exaggerated claims of conspiracy theorists and the hyperbolic tone that typify many of these movies – *The Greatest Lie Ever Sold* (2005) and *Loose Change* (2006), for example – means that they cannot be taken as a serious attempt to engage in historical debate through film. Indeed the evident paranoid tone of these movies may more often have the reverse effect of making the 'official' version appear more plausible.

Here, then, is a role for historically informed film criticism; criticism that can look beneath the seamless narratives and the surface verisimilitude in order to reveal the textual mechanisms through which a film is constructed and the extent to which historical evidence is employed, and how faithfully it is employed, in staging onscreen a visual representation of the past. As Robert Brent Toplin argues, there is little to be gained from merely dismissing the historical film because of its failure to adhere to 'the most exacting standards of scholarship' (1996: 2), but we must also always be alert to

the dangers of too much tolerance. Artistic creativity can be abused. Filmmakers who see no limits to their imagination may present badly distorted pictures of the past. The matter of how much slack is acceptable in the rope of creative liberty remains an intriguing question. (Ibid.)

The task for historically informed criticism now is to engage fully with the historical film, to conceptualise its potential and its limitations and to celebrate progressive examples of historical filmmaking as well as expose those which retain only the most tenuous connection to the events they depict. In making this case I endorse the argument of Pierre Sorlin who concludes that simply ignoring or dismissing the historical film is not an option for historians any longer. Those who do so risk becoming obsolete in a world in which the encounter with social reality is more commonly mediated through audio-visual material than it is experienced directly or through other channels:

if historians today neglect audio-visual material, it will continue to exist in spite of them as a history through pictures. Furthermore, the public will lose all interest in specialists, and the specialists themselves will be in a curiously divided position, conducting their research shut away in libraries, but turning to television when they want information on the present. Historians must take an interest in the audio-visual world, if they are not to become schizophrenic, rejected by society as the representatives of an outmoded erudition. (2001: 26)

We cannot, then, simply turn our backs on the historical film like the more traditional type of historian might prefer to, nor should we succumb to the worst excesses of relativism engendered by postmodernism. Instead film historians must critically engage with each historical film as we find it, praising the meritorious and challenging those that take excessive liberties with historical fact. In the dialogue that thus emerges between historical film and criticism lies the prospect of a valuable syncretic mode of historical knowledge that unites the strengths of both traditional academic written history and the unrivalled verisimilitude attainable in the movies.

NOTES

introduction

1   See Richards (2000) and the introduction to Chapman *et al.* (2007) for succinct accounts of the split.
2   See, for example, Toby Haggith's (2002) comparative analysis of newsreel footage of the D-Day landings with the opening scenes of *Saving Private Ryan*.
3   Colin McArthur's (1998) dissection of the multiple historical inaccuracies in *Braveheart* (1995) is exemplary.
4   The survey also revealed that visits to museums or historical sites were slightly more popular than historical books, attracting 57.2% of those surveyed.

chapter one

1   It was not until 1981 that the leading journal concerned with history and film, *The Historical Journal of Film, Radio and Television*, was established.
2   As Chapman *et al.* observe, most of the serious works of academic historical film scholarship have been written in the last 25 years (2007: 2).
3   In this respect it is necessary to make a distinction between reception studies and audience research, which does involve talking to actual viewers and is typified by the use of ethnographic methods to investigate actual instances of reception.
4   See, for example, Justin Smith's use of 'web ethnography' (2007).
5   Staiger's fifth hypothesis calls for an interdisciplinary approach to the analysis of reception 'events', as she terms them.

6   This is cited by Barbara Klinger, without reference (1997: 109).

7   In effect the version of a historical past provided by the zeitgeist approach amounts to little more than an idealist projection of that past founded on the cultural and political imperatives of the present in which it is formed.

8   For an example of the ability of a film to polarise opinions between different viewers compare Alexander Walker's review of David Fincher's *Fight Club* (1999) for the London Evening Standard – 'it is an inadmissible assault on personal decency. And on society itself' (Walker 1999) – with that of Peter Travers for Rolling Stone – '*Fight Club* pulls you in, challenges your prejudices, rocks your world and leaves you laughing in the face of an abyss. It's alive, all right. It's also an uncompromising American classic' (Travers 1999: 113–14).

9   Some of these characteristics were a feature of other publicity materials for the film: for example 'Bogart and Bacall. In Action! In Danger! In Love!'

10 Although there are other possible sources of this sort of direct evidence of a 'reception event', such as diaries and journals kept by cinemagoers, in practice these are rarely easily obtainable.

11 Determining box office success is itself far from straightforward, however, and can provide a misleading sense of the significance of particular films.

12 See Schatz 1999: 68–78 for an account of the growth of the use of market research in the Hollywood movie industries.

13 For example, Haley 1952, Smythe *et al.* 1955, Wanderer 1970 and Austin et al 1981.

chapter two

1   The categories were: Best Cinematography, Color; Best Director; Best Sound, Recording; Best Writing, Screenplay.

2   The idea that the windows in the apartments across the courtyard from Jefferies' apartment conform to cinematic aspect ratios in use at the time is often invoked by scholars to reinforce the cinematic metaphor of the film. Although this view of the set as a specifically cinematic metaphor has tended to dominate film scholarship, it is worth noting that the pre-eminence of this view has only been achieved at the cost

of 'forgetting' that other ways of conceptualising the setting have been suggested by numerous writers over the years. Belton's argument in his 1988 article is that the film combines elements of cinematic and theatrical spectacle, while Dana Brand argues that the courtyard is 'behaving as a diorama' (1999: 127). John A. Bertolini also sees the courtyard as a theatrical rather than cinematic space, being 'roughly the shape of a proscenium stage' (2002: 235), while John Fawell argues that 'it may be more to the point to see Jeff as a television watcher rather than a filmgoer (2001: 130).

chapter three

1   Letter to the editor of *The American*, 8 April 1915, cited by Lennig (2004: 117)
2   This section of the newspaper publishes readers' queries, to which other readers respond.
3   In this chapter I concentrate on the latter rather than the 'new historicist' critique of traditional historiography. While it is important not to conflate postmodernism and new historicism, both approaches share many similarities and for the purposes of this book the postmodern approach represents, in my view, the more radical and far-reaching challenge to traditional historiography.
4   Hofstadter also recognised the parallels between the activity of historians and the myth-making propensity of the wider population; 'the historian is free to try to dissociate myths from reality, but the same impulse to myth-making that moves his fellow man is also at work in him' (quoted in Brown 2006: xiii).
5   This idea is central to some of the recent important work on historical films. James Chapman's study of the British historical movie, for example, is explicitly a 'study of the way the British historical film has used the past as a means of "talking about" the present' (2005: 2).
6   Whether Wilson actually said this or anything like it is questionable. Although the remark is reported in numerous books and articles in film studies, its provenance is difficult to establish (see Lennig 2004: 122).
7   Although writing may have changed the practice of oral history, facilitating the development of a new sub-genre of written 'oral' histories. See the work of Studs Terkel, for example.

chapter four

1   Quotation taken from document ref DL/7/4, titled 'Possible scenes, sequences, characters or visuals' dated October 1959. British Film Institute David Lean Collection. According to these notes it was intended that Lawrence would speak the line in the film.
2   Document reference DL/7/1 – letter from T. E. Lawrence to Rex Ingram, 21 July 1927. British Film Institute David Lean Collection.
3   T. E. Lawrence died in 1935 as a result of a motorcycle accident.
4   It is only fair to note that there is only a small amount of material relavant to the production of *Lawrence of Arabia* in this collection and it is possible that papers detailing historical research carried out for the film remain to be discovered or else have been destroyed.
5   Document reference DL/7/8 – letter from David Lean to Sam Spiegel, 7 January 1961. British Film Institute David Lean Collection.
6   Ibid.
7   The Five Points intersection no longer exists but the location is part of the area now known as Chinatown.
8   Notably, in the period depicted, Irish Catholics.
9   White protestants born in America.
10 William 'Bill The Butcher' Cutting is perhaps the most notable example in the film of a character who is based on a person who lived in the Five Points around the time in question. The character is loosely based on Bill Poole, a local 'sporting man' and Whig politician, who was actually killed in 1855, seven years before the date set for the main part of the film.
11 Publicity soundbite used in National Public Radio show *All Things Considered*, feature on *Gangs of New York*, 23 December 2002. Reproduced on History News Network website, http://hnn.us/comments/6212.html. Accessed 26 July 2006. Hereafter referred to as HNN.
12 Many of the artefacts were later lost again when the World Trade Center, which housed them, was destroyed in 2001.
13 *Radio Times* show on WHYY, Philadelphia, 1 June 2003. Http://www.whyy.org/cgi-bin/newwebRTsearcher.cgi. Accessed 31 July 2006.
14 The author, Charles Dickens, visited the neighbourhood in 1842, and published a detailed account of the degradation he found in the district. See Anbinder 2002: 32–4 for details of Dickens's and other 'slumming' visits to the Five Points.

15 The Chinese nightclub was a real place in the Five Points neighbour-hood, although it was not built until 1870, seven years after the draft riots that are depicted at the end the movie.

16 *Radio Times* show on WHYY, Philadelphia, 1 June 2003. Http://www.whyy.org/cgi-bin/newwebRTsearcher.cgi. Accessed 31 July 2006.

17 See the History News Network website, http://hnn.us/comments/6212.html. Accessed 26 July 2006.

chapter five

1 The report of the 9/11 Commission evidently informs all of the films based on the events relating to United Airlines flight 93.

FILMOGRAPHY

24 (Fox TV, 2001–present, US)
A Clockwork Orange (Stanley Kubrick, 1971, UK)
The Big Sleep (Howard Hawks, 1946, US)
The Birth of a Nation (D. W. Griffith, 1915, US)
Braveheart (Mel Gibson, 1995, US)
Bridge of the River Kwai (David Lean, 1957, UK/US)
Fight Club (David Fincher, 1999, US)
Flight 93 (Fox TV, 2006, US)
The Flight That Fought Back (Discovery Channel, 2005, US)
Gangs of New York (Martin Scorsese, 2002, US)
Good Night, and Good Luck (George Clooney, 2005, US)
The Greatest Lie Ever Sold (Anthony J. Hilder, 2005, US)
Lawrence of Arabia (David Lean, 1962, UK)
Let's Roll: The Story of Flight 93 (Granada TV, 2002, UK)
Loose Change (Dylan Avery, 2005, US)
Munich (Steven Spielberg, 2005, US)
North By Northwest (Alfred Hitchcock, 1959, US)
Oliver Twist (David Lean, 1948, UK)
Perry Mason (CBS TV, 1957–66, US)
Picnic (Joshua Logan, 1955, US)
Rear Window (Alfred Hitchcock, 1954, US)
Saving Private Ryan (Steven Spielberg, 1998, US)
The Shanghai Gesture (Josef von Sternberg, 1941, US)
Troy (Wolfgang Petersen, 2004, US)
United 93 (Paul Greengrass, 2006, Fr/UK/US)
The Wild Bunch (Sam Peckinpah, 1969, US)
World Trade Center: Anatomy of the Collapse (Learning Channel, 2002, US)
World Trade Center (Oliver Stone, 2006, US)

BIBLIOGRAPHY

Aldington, R. (1971) *Lawrence of Arabia: A Biographical Inquiry.* Harmondsworth: Penguin.

Allen, R. C. and D. Gomery (1985) *Film History: Theory and Practice.* New York: McGraw Hill .

Allen, R. C. (1998) 'From Exhibition to Reception: Reflections on the Audience in Film History', in A. Kuhn and J. Stacey (eds) *Screen Histories: A Screen Reader.* Oxford, Clarendon Press: 13–21.

____ (2006) 'Relocating American film history: the 'problem' of the empirical', *Cultural Studies* 20, 1, 48–88.

Althusser, L. (2001) *Lenin and Philosophy and Other Essays.* New York: Monthly Review Press.

Anbinder, T. (2002) *Five Points: The 19th Century New York City Neighborhood that Invented Tap Dance, Stole Elections and Became the World's Most Notorious Slum.* New York: Plume.

Anon. (1944a) 'The Weaker sex is – Male', *Science Digest* 15, 4, April, 1–4.

____ (1944b) 'Male and Female', *Time*, 23 October, 55.

____ (1945) 'How Much Do You Know about Men?', *Readers Digest*, April, 23–4.

____ (1955) 'All-Time Top Grossers', *Variety*, 5 January, 59, 63.

____ (2002) 'Is Gangs of New York Historically Accurate?', *Gotham Gazette*, 23 December. Http://www.gothamgazette.com/article/20021223/202/162. Accessed 30 July 2006.

____ (2003) *Martin Scorsese's Gangs of New York: Making the Movie.* London: Headline.

____ (2004) 'Notes and Queries', *Guardian*, 10 November, 17.

Armes, R. (1981) *Problems of Film History.* London: Curriculum Centre for the History of Art and Design in association with the British Film Institute.

Asbury, H. (2002) *The Gangs of New York: An Informal History of the Underworld.* London: Arrow Books.

Austin, B. A., M. J. Nicolich and T. Simonet (1981) 'M.P.A.A. Ratings and the
     Box Office: Some Tantalizing Statistics', *Film Quarterly* 35, 2, 28–30.
Barta, T. (ed.) (1998) *Screening the Past: Film and the Representation of
     History*. London: Praeger.
Barthes, R. (1990) *S/Z*. Oxford: Blackwell.
Bartolomeo, L. (2003) 'Rewriting History: Professor Tyler Anbinder's research
     plays a key role in Scorsese's', *GW Hatchet Online: An Independent
     Student Newspaper*. Washington D. C. Http://www.gwhatchet.com/
     media/storage/paper332/news/2003/01/21/Features/Rewriting.
     History-347693.shtml. Accessed 31 July 2006.
Barton-Palmer, R. (1986) 'The Metafictional Hichcock: The Experience of
     Viewing and the Viewing of Experience in *Rear Window* and *Psycho*',
     Cinema Journal 25, 2, 4–19.
Belton, J. (1988) 'The Space of Rear Window', *Modern Language Notes* 103, 5,
     1121–38.
_____ (2000) 'Spectacle and Narrative', in J. Belton (ed.) *Alfred Hitchcock's
     Rear Window*. Cambridge: Cambridge University Press, 1–20.
Bennett, T. (1982) 'Text and Social Process: The Case of James Bond', *Screen
     Education* 41, 3–14.
Bertolini, J. A. (2002) 'Rear Window, or the Reciprocated Glance', in
     S. Gottleib and C. Brookhouse (eds) *Framing Hitchcock*. Detroit: Wayne
     State University Press, 234–50.
Black, G. (1995) 'Film History and Film Archives', *Literature Film Quarterly* 23,
     2, 102.
Bordwell, D. (1997) *On The History of Film Style*. Cambridge, MA: Harvard
     University Press.
Bordwell, D. and K. Thompson (2003) *Film History: An Introduction*. New York:
     McGraw Hill.
Bottomore, S. (1994) 'Out of This World: Theory, Fact and Film History', *Film
     History* 6, 1, 7–25.
Brand, D. (1999) 'Rear-View Mirror: Hitchcock, Poe and the Flaneur in
     America', in J. Freedman and R. Millington (eds) *Hitchcock's America*.
     Oxford: Oxford University Press, 123–34.
Braudy, L. and M. Cohen (eds) (1999) *Film Theory and Criticism: Introductory
     Readings*. Oxford: Oxford University Press.
Briley, R. (2002) 'Teaching Film and History', *Magazine of History* 16, 4, 3–4.
Brown, D. (2006) *Richard Hofstadter: An Intellectual Biography*. Chicago:
     University of Chicago Press.

Browne, A. R. and L. A. Kreiser Jr (2003) 'The Civil War and Reconstruction', in P. C. Rollins (ed.) *The Columbia Companion to American History on Film*. New York: Columbia University Press, 58–68.

Brownlow, K. (1997) *David Lean*. London: Faber and Faber.

Buckland, W. (2003) 'A new cultural history of film', *Semiotica* 145, 1/4, 281–8.

Burgoyne, R. (1998) 'Film Nation: Hollywood Looks at U.S. History', *Journalism and Mass Communication Quarterly* 75, 1, 210.

Cameron, K. M. (1997) *America on Film: Hollywood and American History*. New York: Continuum.

Capussotti, E., G. Lauricella and L. Passerini (2004) 'Film as a Source for Cultural History: an Experiment in Practical Methodology', *History Workshop Journal* 57, 1, 256–62.

Carr, E. H. (1990) *What is History?* London: Penguin Books.

Carrier, R. C. (2002) 'The Function of the Historian in Society', *The History Teacher* 35, 4. Http://www.historycooperative.org/journals/ht/35.4/carrier.html. Accessed 29 May 2008.

Carroll, N. (1996) 'Film History and Film Theory: An Outline for an Institutional Theory of Film', in *Theorizing the Moving Image*. Cambridge: Cambridge University Press, 375–91.

Carter, E. (1998) 'Cultural History Written with Lightning: The Significance of *The Birth of a Nation* (1915)' in P. C. Rollins (ed.) *Hollywood as Historian: American Film in a Cultural Context*. Lexington: The University Press of Kentucky, 9–19.

Cartmell, D., I. Q. Hunter and I. Whelehan (2001) *Retrovisions: Reinventing the Past in Film and Fiction*. London: Pluto Press.

Chamberlain, T. (2003). 'Gangs of New York: Fact vs. Fiction', *National Geographic News*, 24 March. Http://news.nationalgeographic.com/news/2003/03/0320_030320_oscars_gangs.html. Accessed 31 July 2006.

Chambers, J. W. and D. Culbert (eds) (1998) *World War II, Film and History*. Oxford: Oxford University Press.

Chapman, J. (2005) *Past and Present: National Identity and the British Historical Film*. London: I B Tauris.

Chapman, J., M. Glancy and S. Harper (eds) (2007) *The New Film History: Sources, Methods, Approaches*. Basingstoke: Palgrave Macmillan.

Chion, M. (2000) 'Alfred Hitchcock's *Rear Window*: The Fourth Side', in J. Belton (ed.) *Alfred Hitchcock's Rear Window*. Cambridge: Cambridge University Press, 110–17.

Cohan, S. (1997) *Masked Men: Masculinity and the Movies in the Fifties*. Bloomington: Indiana University Press.

_____ (2003). 'An Innocent Eye: The "Pictorial Turn", Film Studies, History', *History of Education Quarterly* 43, 2, 250–61.

Collins, R. (2003) 'Concealing the Poverty of Traditional Historiography: myth as mystification in historical discourse', *Rethinking History* 7, 3, 341–65.

Comolli, J.-L. and J. Narboni (1972) 'John Ford's *Young Mr. Lincoln*', *Screen* 13, 3, 5–44.

_____ (1999) 'Cinema/Ideology/Criticism', in L. Braudy and M. Cohen (eds) *Film Theory and Criticism: Introductory Readings*. Oxford: Oxford University Press, 752–9.

Cook, P. (2005) *Screening the Past: Memory and Nostalgia in Cinema*. London and New York: Routledge.

Corrigan, P. (1983) 'Film Entertainment as Ideology and Pleasure: a Preliminary Approach to a History of Audiences', in J. Curran and V. Porter (eds) *British Cinema History*. London: British Film Institute, 24–35.

Curtis, S. (2000) 'The Making of *Rear Window*', in J. Belton (ed.) *Alfred Hitchcock's Rear Window*. Cambridge: Cambridge University Press, 21–46.

Dabashi, H. (2006) 'Native informers and the making of the American empire', *Al Ahram online*. Http://weekly.ahram.org.eg/2006/797/special. htm. Accessed 15 December 2006.

Daddow, O. J. (2004) 'The Ideology of Apathy: Historians and Postmodernism', *Rethinking History* 8, 3, 417–37.

Dawson, G. (1984). 'History Writing on World War II', in G. Hurd (ed.) *National Fictions: World War 2 in British Films and Television*. London: British Film Institute, 1–7.

Demos, J. (2005) 'Afterword: Notes From, and About, the History/Fiction Borderland', *Rethinking History* 9, 2/3, 329–35.

Deutelbaum, M. and L. Poague (eds) (1986) *A Hitchcock Reader*. Ames, Iowa: Iowa State University Press.

DiGirolamo, V. (2004) 'Such, Such Were the *B'hoys*', *Radical History Review* 90, 123–41.

Doane, M. A. (1990) 'Response', *Camera Obscura* 20, 1, 142–7.

Douchet, J. (1986 [1960]) 'Hitch and His Public', in M. Deutelbaum and L. Poague (eds) *A Hitchcock Reader*. Ames, Iowa: Iowa State University Press, 7–15.

Eco, U. (1981) *The Role of the Reader: Explorations in the Semiotics of Texts*. London: Hutchinson.

Elsaesser, T. (1987) 'Cinema – The Irresponsible Signifier or "The Gamble With History": Film Theory or Cinema Theory', *New German Critique* 40, 65–89.

Fawall, J. (2001) *Hitchcock's Rear Window: The Well-Made Film*. Carbondale: Southern Illinois University Press.

Finney, P. (2005) 'Who Speaks for History?', *Rethinking History* 9, 4, 503–19.

Fletcher, I. C. (2002) 'Film and History', *Radical History Review* 83, 173–4.

Freedman, J. and R. Millington (eds) (1999) *Hitchcock's America*. Oxford: Oxford University Press.

Fukuyama, F. (1992) *The End of History and the Last Man*. New York: The Free Press.

Fullerton, J. (ed.) (2004) *Screen Culture: History and Textuality*. London: John Libbey.

Geraghty, C. (2000) *British Cinema in the Fifties: Gender, Genre and the New Look*. London: Routledge.

Gilje, P. (2003) 'Gangs, the Five Points, and the American Public.' *Common-Place* 3, 4, July. Http://www.historycooperative.org/journals/cp/vol-03/no-04/reviews/gilje.shtml. Accessed 26 July 2006.

Gomery, D. (1998 [1976]) 'Writing the History of the American Film Industry: Warner Brothers and Sound', in A. Kuhn and J. Stacey (eds) *Screen Histories: A Screen Reader*. Oxford: Clarendon Press: 139–47.

Haggith, T. (2002) 'D-Day Filming – For Real. A Comparison of 'truth' and 'reality' in *Saving Private Ryan* and combat film by the British Army's Film and Photographic Unit', *Film History* 14, 3/4, 332–53.

Haley, J. (1952) 'The Appeal of the Moving Picture', *Quarterly of Film, Radio and Television* 6, 4, 361–74.

Hall, S. (1996) 'Encoding/Decoding', in S. Hall, D. Hobson, A. Lowe and P. Willis (eds) *Culture, Media, Language*. London: Routledge: 128–38.

Handel, L. (1950) *Hollywood Looks at its Audience: A Report of Film Audience Research*. Urbana: University of Illinois Press.

Hansen, M. (1991) *Babel and Babylon: Spectatorship in American Silent Film*. Cambridge, MA: Harvard University Press.

Harper, S. (2004) 'Film History: Beyond the Archive?', *Journal of Contemporary History* 39, 447–54.

Heath, S. (1975a) 'Film and System, Terms of Analysis Part 1', *Screen* 16, 1, 7–77.

Heath, S. (1975b) 'Film and System, Terms of Analysis Part 2', *Screen* 16, 2, 91–113.

Higashi, S. (1998) 'Rethinking Film as American History', *Rethinking History* 2, 1, 87–102.

_____ (2004) 'In Focus: Film History, or a Baedeker Guide to the Historical Turn', *Cinema Journal* 44, 1, 94–143.

Irving, D (1991) *Hitler's War*. London: Focal Point.

Iser, W. (1974) *The Implied Reader: Patterns of Communication in Prose Fiction from Bunyan to Beckett*. Baltimore: Johns Hopkins University Press.

Jameson, F. (1989) *The Political Unconscious: Narrative as a Socially Significant Act*. London: Routledge.

_____ (1991) *Postmodernism or, the Cultural Logic of Late Capitalism*. Durham: Duke University Press.

Jarvie, I. (1978) 'Seeing Through the Movies', *Philosophy of the Social Sciences* 8, 4, 374–97.

Jauss, H. R. (1970) 'Literary History as a Challenge to Literary Theory', *New Literary History* 2, 1, 7–37.

_____ (1982) *Toward an Aesthetic of Reception*. Minneapolis: University of Minnesota Press.

Jenkins, K. (2004) 'Modernist Disavowals and Postmodern Reminders of the Condition of History Today: on Jean Francois Lyotard', *Rethinking History* 8, 3, 365–85.

Kapsis, R. E. (1992) *Hitchcock: The Making of a Reputation*. Chicago: University of Chicago Press.

Katz, E. (1959) 'Mass Communication Research and the Study of Popular Culture: An editorial note on a possible future for this journal', *Studies in Public Communication* 2, 1–6.

Kinsey, A. C., W. C. Pomeroy and C. E. Martin (1948) *Sexual Behaviour in the Human Male*. Philadelphia: W. B. Saunders Co.

Kinsey, A. C., W. C. Pomeroy, C. E. Martin and P. H. Gebhard (1953) *Sexual Behaviour in the Human Female*. Philadelphia and London: W. B. Saunders.

King, G. (2005) ' "Just Like A Movie"?: 9/11 and Hollywood Spectacle', in G. King (ed.) *The Spectacle of the Real: From Hollywood to Reality TV and Beyond*. Bristol: Intellect Press, 47–57.

Klinger, B. (1997) 'Film history terminable and interminable: recovering the past in reception studies', *Screen* 38, 2, 107–28.

Kuhn, A. and J. Stacey (eds) (1998a) *Screen Histories: A Screen Reader*. Oxford: Clarendon Press.

Kuhn, A. and J. Stacey (1998b) 'Screen Histories: An Introduction', in *Screen Histories: A Screen Reader*. Oxford: Clarendon Press, 1–10.

Kunz, D. (2001) 'History, Film, and the "Cinematic Historian"', *Literature Film Quarterly* 29, 1, 71–2.

Lacan, J. (1977) *Ecrits: A Selection*. London: Tavistock Press.

Landy, M. (1996) *Cinematic Uses of the Past*. Minneapolis: University of Minnesota Press.

Landy, M. (ed.) (2001) *The Historical Film: History and Memory in Media*. London: The Athlone Press.

Lawrence, T. E. (1962) *Seven Pillars of Wisdom*. Harmondsworth: Penguin.

Lemire, E. (2000) 'Voyeurism and the Postwar Crisis of Masculinity in Rear Window', in J. Belton (ed.) *Alfred Hitchcock's Rear Window*. Cambridge: Cambridge University Press, 57–90.

Lennig, A. (2004) 'Myth and Fact: The Reception of *The Birth of a Nation*', *Film History* 16, 117–41.

Lezard, N. (2006) 'Official: Men Are the Frailer Sex', *Guardian*, 3 March, 22.

Litwack, L. F. (1996) '*The Birth of a Nation*', in T. Mico, J. Miller-Monzon and D. Rubel (eds) *Past Imperfect: History According to the Movies*. New York: Henry Holt and Company, 136–41.

Lukacs, G. (1974) *The Historical Novel*. London: Merlin Press.

Maltby, R. (1992) 'Film Noir and the Politics of the Maladjusted Text', in I. Cameron (ed.) *The Movie Book of Film Noir*. London: Studio Vista: 39–48.

McArthur, C. (1998) '*Braveheart* and the Scottish Aesthetic Dementia', in T. Barta (ed.) *Screening the Past: Film and the Representation of History*. Westport, CT: Praeger.

McCrisken, T. and A. Pepper (2005) *American History and Contemporary Hollywood Film*. Edinburgh: Edinburgh University Press.

Miller, W. R. (2003) 'New York City's mid-19th century underworld: a history, a novel, a film', *Crime History and Societies* 7, 2, 103–6.

Modleski, T. (1988) *The Women Who Knew Too Much*. London and New York: Methuen.

Morley, D. (1980) *The Nationwide Audience: Structure and Decoding*. London: British Film Institute.

Mulvey, L. (1999 [1975]) 'Visual Pleasure and Narrative Cinema' in L. Braudy and M. Cohen (eds) *Film Theory and Criticism: Introductory Readings*. Oxford: Oxford University Press, 833–44.

Naish, J. (2005) 'Who's a Pretty Boy?; Breakthroughs, Tips and Trends,' *Times*, 10 December, 3.

Naremore, J. (1995) 'American Film Noir: The History of an Idea', *Film Quarterly* 49, 2, 12–29.

National Commission on Terrorist Attacks upon the United States (2004) *The 9/11 Commission Report*. New York and London: W. W. Norton.

Neale, S. (2000) *Genre and Hollywood*. London: Routledge.

O'Connor, J. and M. Jackson (eds) (1988) *American History/American Film: Interpreting the Hollywood Image*. New York: Continuum.

Pinhey, L. (2002). 'Using Film to Teach History: An ERIC/ChESS Sample', *Magazine of History* 16, 4, 45–7.

Rebhorn, M. (1988) *Screening America: Using Hollywood Films to Teach History*. New York: Peter Lang.

Richards, Jeffrey (1973) *Visions of Yesterday*. London and New York: Routledge.

____ (1984) *The Age of the Dream Palace*. London and New York: Routledge.

____ (2000) 'Rethinking British Cinema', in J. Ashby and A. Higson (eds) *British Cinema, Past and Present*. London and New York: Routledge, 21–34.

Rollins, P. C. (ed.) (1998) *Hollywood as Historian: American Film in a Cultural Context*. Lexington: University Press of Kentucky.

____ (ed.) (2003). *The Columbia Companion to History on Film*. New York: Columbia University Press.

Rosenstone, R. (1988) 'History in Images/History in Words: Reflections on the Possibility of Really Putting History onto Film', *American Historical Review* 93,5, 1173–85.

____ (1996a) 'The Crisis of History/The Promise of Film', *Media International Australia*, 80, 5–11.

____ (1996b) 'The Future of the Past: Film and the Beginning of Postmodern History', in V. Sobchack (ed.) *The Persistence of History: Cinema, Television, and the Modern Event*. New York and London: Routledge: 201–18.

____ (1996c) *Visions of the Past: The Challenge of Film to Our Idea of History*. Cambridge, MA: Harvard University Press.

____ (2004a) 'Inventing Historical Truth on the Silver Screen', *Cineaste* 29, 2, 29–33.

____ (2004b) 'Confessions of a Postmodern (?) Historian', *Rethinking History* 8,1, 149–66.

Rosenzweig, R. (2000) 'Popular Uses of History in the United States: Professional Historians and Popular Historymakers', *Perspectives* 38, 5, May. Http://www.historians.org/perspectives/issues/2000/0005/0005spl2.cfm. Accessed 23 June 2006.

Samuels, R. (1998) *Hitchcock's Bi-Textuality: Lacan, Feminisms, and Queer Theory*. Albany: SUNY Press.

Sante, L. (1991) *Low Life: The Lures and Snares of Old New York*. New York: Farrar, Strauss, Giroux.

Schatz, T. (1999) *Boom and Bust: American Cinema in the 1940s*. Berkeley: University of California Press.

Schneider, R. A. (2006) 'On Film Reviews in the AHR', *Perspectives* 44, 5, May. Http://www.historians.org/Perspectives/issues/2006/0605/0605aha2.cfm. Accessed 20 October 2006.

Sharff, S. (2000) *The Art of Looking in Hitchcock's Rear Window*. New York: Limelight Editions.

Simons, J. D. (ed.) (1990) *Literature and Film in the Historical Dimension*. Gainesville: University Press of Florida.

Slotkin, R. (2005) 'Fiction for the Purposes of History', *Rethinking History* 9, 2/3, 221–36.

Smith, J. (2007) 'The Wicker Man (1973) Email Digest: A Case Study in Web Ethnography', in J. Chapman, M. Glancy and S. Harper (eds) *The New Film History: Sources, Methods, Approaches*. Basingstoke: Palgrave Macmillan, 229–44.

Smythe, D. W., J. R. Gregory, A. Ostrin, O. P. Colvin and W. Moroney (1955) 'Portrait of a First Run Audience', *Quarterly of Film, Radio and Television* 9, 4, 390–409.

Sorlin, P. (1980) *The Film in History: Restaging the Past*. Oxford: Basil Blackwell.

_____ (2001). 'How to look at an 'historical' film', in M. Landy (ed.) *The Historical Film: History and Memory in Media*. London: The Athlone Press, 25–49.

Spicer, A. (2004) 'Film Studies and the Turn to History', *Journal of Contemporary History* 39, 1, 147–56.

Stalger, J. (1985) 'The Politics of Film Canons', *Cinema Journal* 24, 3, 4–23.

_____ (1992) *Interpreting Films: Studies in the Historical Reception of American Cinema*. Princeton, NJ: Princeton University Press.

_____ (2000) *Perverse Spectators: The Practices of Film Reception*. New York: New York University Press.

_____ (2001). 'Writing the History of American Film Reception', in M. Stokes and R. Maltby (eds) *Hollywood Spectatorship: Changing Perceptions of Cinema Audiences*. London: British Film Institute.

_____ (2005). *Media Reception Studies*. New York: New York University Press.

Stam, R. and R. Pearson (1986 [1983]) 'Hitchcock's *Rear Window*: Reflexivity and the Critique of Voyeurism', in M. Deutelbaum and L. Poague (eds) *A Hitchcock Reader*. Ames, Iowa: Iowa State University Press: 193–206.

Talens, J. and S. Zunzunegui (1997) 'Toward a "True" History of Cinema: Film History as Narration', *Boundary 2*, 24, 1, 1–34.

Thomas, L. (Undated) *With Lawrence in Arabia*. London: Hutchinson and Co.

Thumim, J. (1992) *Celluloid Sisters: Women and Popular Cinema*. Basingstoke: Macmillan.

Todorov, T. (1990) *Genres in Discourse*. Cambridge: Cambridge University Press.

Toplin, R. B. (1996) *History by Hollywood: The Use and Abuse of the American Past*. Urbana: University of Illinois Press.

Toplin, R. B. (2002) 'Invigorating History: Using Film in the Classroom', *Magazine of History* 16, 4, 5–6.

Travers, P. (1999) '*Fight Club*', *Rolling Stone*, 28 October, 113–14.

Truffaut, F. (1986) *Hitchcock*. New York: Simon and Schuster.

Turner, A. (1999) *Robert Bolt: Scenes From Two Lives*. London: Vintage.

Usai, P. C. (1994) 'The Philosophy of Film History', *Film History* 6, 1, 3–5.

Walker, A. (1999) '*Fight Club*', *Evening Standard*, 11 November. Http:// www.compsoc.man.ac.uk/~heather/mustard/walker.htm. Accessed 16 February 2005.

Wanderer, J. (1970) 'In Defense of Popular Taste: Film Ratings Among Professionals and Lay Audiences', *American Journal of Sociology* 76, 2, 262–72.

Weinstein, P. B. (2001) 'Movies as the Gateway to History: The History and Film Project', *History Teacher* 35, 1, 27–48.

White, A. (2000) 'Eternal Vigilance in Rear Window', in J. Belton (ed.) *Alfred Hitchcock's Rear Window*. Cambridge: Cambridge University Press, 57–90.

White, H. (1978) *Tropics of Discourse: Essays in Cultural Criticism*. Baltimore: Johns Hopkins University Press.

_____ (1987) *The Content of the Form*. Baltimore: Johns Hopkins University Press.

_____ (1988) 'Historiography and Historiophoty', *American Historical Review* 93, 5, 1193–9.

_____ (1989) *The Content of the Form: Narrative Discourse and Historical Representation*. Baltimore: Johns Hopkins University Press.

_____ (2005) 'Introduction: Historical Fiction,Fictional History, and Historical Reality', *Rethinking History* 9, 2/3, 147–57.

Wilcox, L. (2005) 'Don DeLillo's *Libra*: History as Text, History as Trauma', *Rethinking History* 9, 2/3, 337–53.

Wilson, J. (2006) *Lawrence of Arabia or Smith in the Desert? David Lean's Film Viewed as History*. Http://www.telstudies.org/film/index.htm. Accessed 30 September 2006.

Wilson, W. (1918) *A History of the American People*. London: Harper and Brothers.

Wood, R. (1986) 'Male Desire, Male Anxiety: The Essential Hitchcock', in M. Deutelbaum and L. Poague (eds) *A Hitchcock Reader*. Ames, Iowa: Iowa State University Press, 219–30.

____ (2002) *Hitchcock's Films Revisited*. New York: Columbia University Press.

Wyke, M. (1997) *Projecting the Past: Ancient Rome, Cinema and History*. New York and London: Routledge.

INDEX